D1622215

HAMMOND

Atlas of the MIDDLE EAST

and

Northern Africa

Mapmakers for the 21st Century

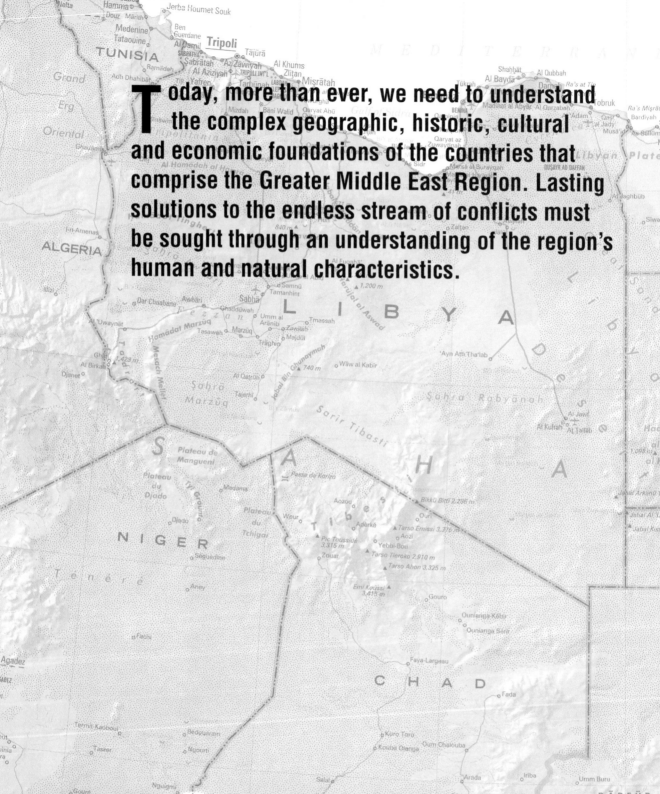

Today, more than ever, we need to understand the complex geographic, historic, cultural and economic foundations of the countries that comprise the Greater Middle East Region. Lasting solutions to the endless stream of conflicts must be sought through an understanding of the region's human and natural characteristics.

Library of Congress Catalog Card Number: 2006921373

ISBN 9-780843-70911-7

PRINTED IN CANADA

Contents

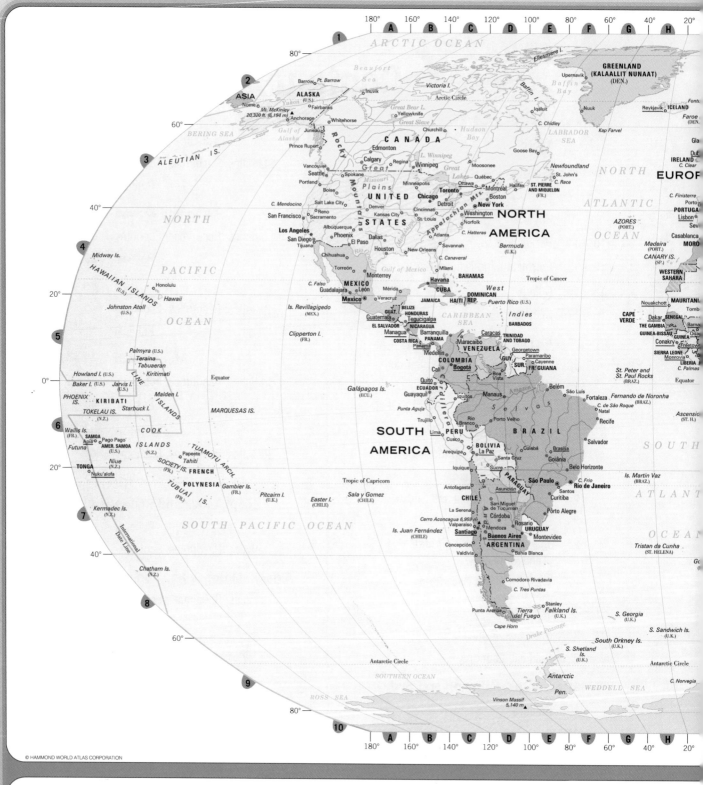

© HAMMOND WORLD ATLAS CORPORATION

United Nations Members

Afghanistan	Azerbaijan	Bosnia and	Central African	Croatia	Equatorial Guinea	Grenada	Ireland
Albania	Bahamas	Herzegovina	Republic	Cuba	Eritrea	Guatemala	Israel
Algeria	Bahrain	Botswana	Chad	Cyprus	Estonia	Guinea	Italy
Andorra	Bangladesh	Brazil	Chile	Czech Republic	Ethiopia	Guinea-Bissau	Jamaica
Angola	Barbados	Brunei	China	Denmark	Fiji	Guyana	Japan
Antigua and	Belarus	Bulgaria	Colombia	Djibouti	Finland	Haiti	Jordan
Barbuda	Belgium	Burkina	Comoros	Dominica	France	Honduras	Kazakhstan
Argentina	Belize	Faso	Congo, Democratic	Dominican	Gabon	Hungary	Kenya
Armenia	Benin	Burundi	Republic of the	Republic	Gambia	Iceland	Kiribati
Australia	Bhutan	Cambodia	Congo,	East Timor	Georgia	India	Kuwait
Austria	Bolivia	Cameroon	Republic of the	Ecuador	Germany	Indonesia	Kyrgyzstan
		Canada	Costa Rica	Egypt	Ghana	Iran	Laos
		Cape Verde	Côte d'Ivoire	El Salvador	Greece	Iraq	Latvia

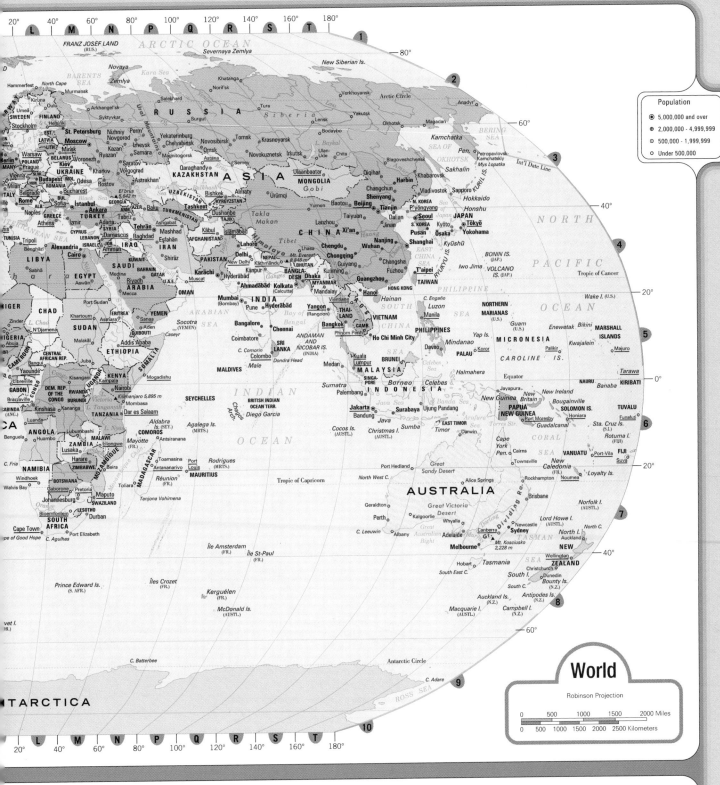

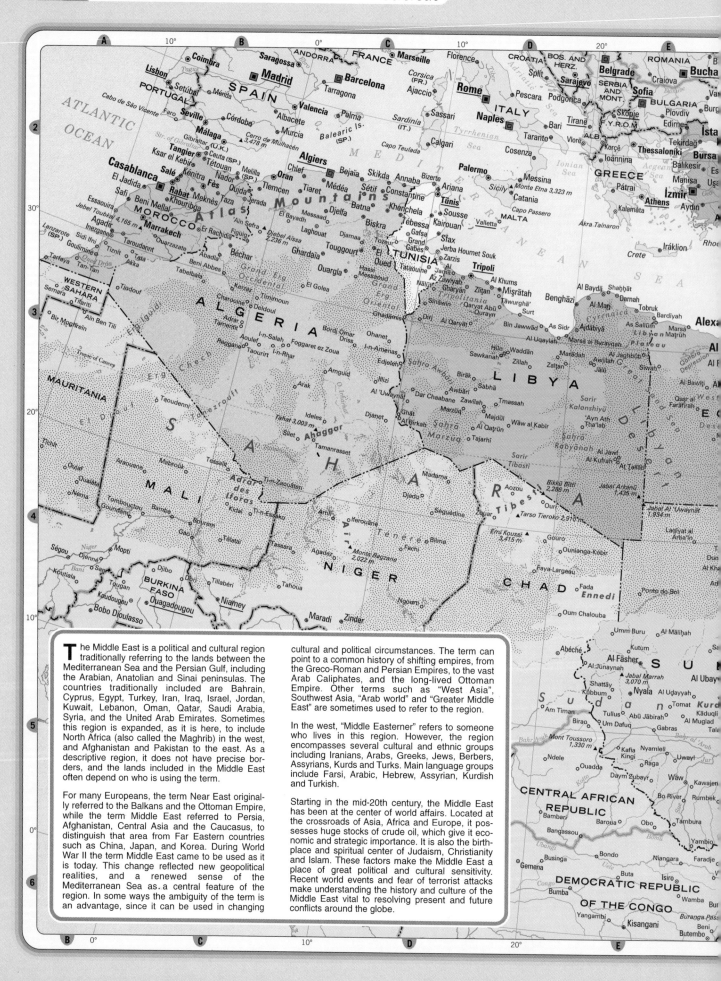

The Middle East is a political and cultural region traditionally referring to the lands between the Mediterranean Sea and the Persian Gulf, including the Arabian, Anatolian and Sinai peninsulas. The countries traditionally included are Bahrain, Cyprus, Egypt, Turkey, Iran, Iraq, Israel, Jordan, Kuwait, Lebanon, Oman, Qatar, Saudi Arabia, Syria, and the United Arab Emirates. Sometimes this region is expanded, as it is here, to include North Africa (also called the Maghrib) in the west, and Afghanistan and Pakistan to the east. As a descriptive region, it does not have precise borders, and the lands included in the Middle East often depend on who is using the term.

For many Europeans, the term Near East originally referred to the Balkans and the Ottoman Empire, while the term Middle East referred to Persia, Afghanistan, Central Asia and the Caucasus, to distinguish that area from Far Eastern countries such as China, Japan, and Korea. During World War II the term Middle East came to be used as it is today. This change reflected new geopolitical realities, and a renewed sense of the Mediterranean Sea as a central feature of the region. In some ways the ambiguity of the term is an advantage, since it can be used in changing cultural and political circumstances. The term can point to a common history of shifting empires, from the Greco-Roman and Persian Empires, to the vast Arab Caliphates, and the long-lived Ottoman Empire. Other terms such as "West Asia", Southwest Asia, "Arab world" and "Greater Middle East" are sometimes used to refer to the region.

In the west, "Middle Easterner" refers to someone who lives in this region. However, the region encompasses several cultural and ethnic groups including Iranians, Arabs, Greeks, Jews, Berbers, Assyrians, Kurds and Turks. Main language groups include Farsi, Arabic, Hebrew, Assyrian, Kurdish and Turkish.

Starting in the mid-20th century, the Middle East has been at the center of world affairs. Located at the crossroads of Asia, Africa and Europe, it possesses huge stocks of crude oil, which give it economic and strategic importance. It is also the birthplace and spiritual center of Judaism, Christianity and Islam. These factors make the Middle East a place of great political and cultural sensitivity. Recent world events and fear of terrorist attacks make understanding the history and culture of the Middle East vital to resolving present and future conflicts around the globe.

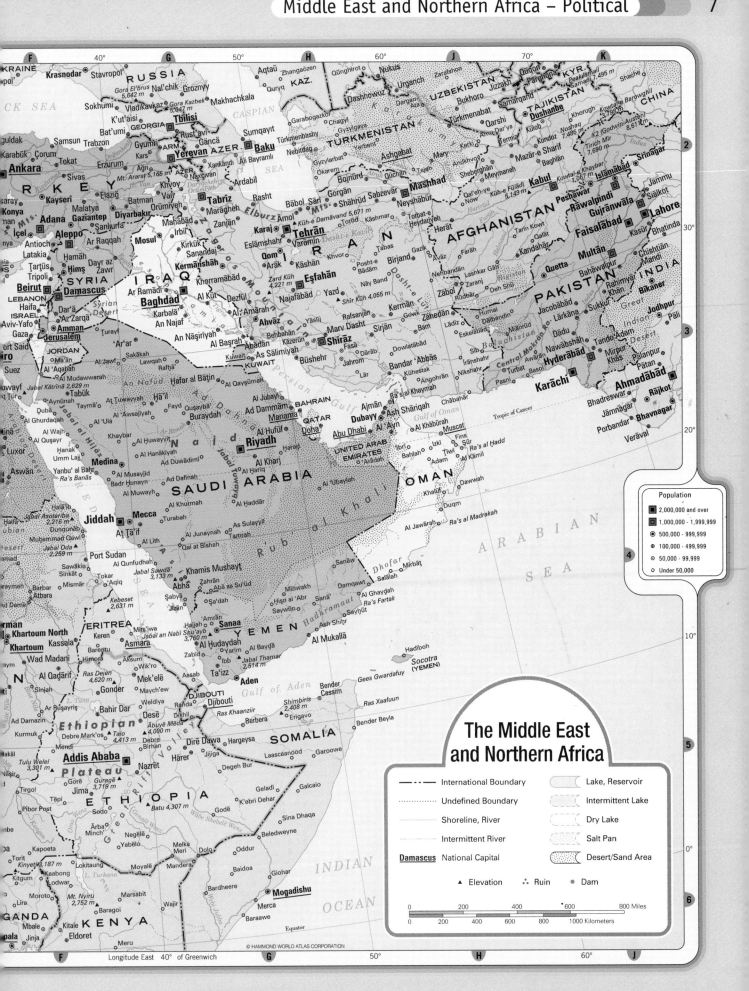

The Middle East
and Northern Africa

─ · ─ · ─ International Boundary	Lake, Reservoir
·········· Undefined Boundary	Intermittent Lake
──── Shoreline, River	Dry Lake
─ · ─ · ─ Intermittent River	Salt Pan
Damascus National Capital	Desert/Sand Area

▲ Elevation   ∴ Ruin   ● Dam

Population	
■	2,000,000 and over
▣	1,000,000 - 1,999,999
◉	500,000 - 999,999
⊕	100,000 - 499,999
⊙	50,000 - 99,999
○	Under 50,000

0   200   400   600   800 Miles
0   200   400   600   800   1000 Kilometers

© HAMMOND WORLD ATLAS CORPORATION

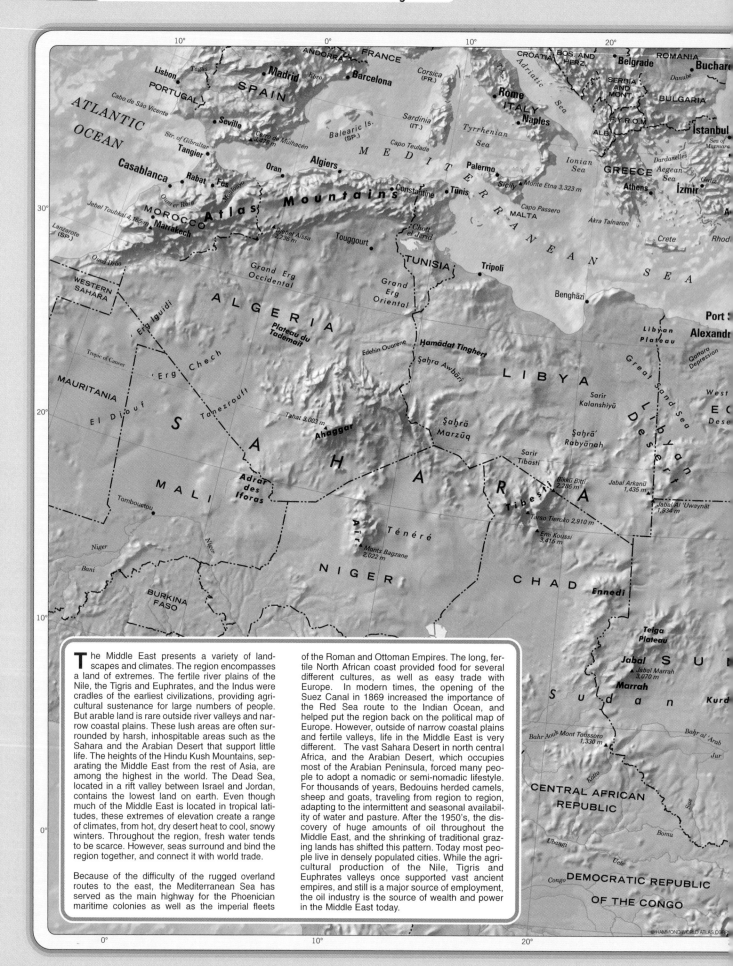

The Middle East presents a variety of land-scapes and climates. The region encompasses a land of extremes. The fertile river plains of the Nile, the Tigris and Euphrates, and the Indus were cradles of the earliest civilizations, providing agricultural sustenance for large numbers of people. But arable land is rare outside river valleys and narrow coastal plains. These lush areas are often surrounded by harsh, inhospitable areas such as the Sahara and the Arabian Desert that support little life. The heights of the Hindu Kush Mountains, separating the Middle East from the rest of Asia, are among the highest in the world. The Dead Sea, located in a rift valley between Israel and Jordan, contains the lowest land on earth. Even though much of the Middle East is located in tropical latitudes, these extremes of elevation create a range of climates, from hot, dry desert heat to cool, snowy winters. Throughout the region, fresh water tends to be scarce. However, seas surround and bind the region together, and connect it with world trade.

Because of the difficulty of the rugged overland routes to the east, the Mediterranean Sea has served as the main highway for the Phoenician maritime colonies as well as the imperial fleets of the Roman and Ottoman Empires. The long, fertile North African coast provided food for several different cultures, as well as easy trade with Europe. In modern times, the opening of the Suez Canal in 1869 increased the importance of the Red Sea route to the Indian Ocean, and helped put the region back on the political map of Europe. However, outside of narrow coastal plains and fertile valleys, life in the Middle East is very different. The vast Sahara Desert in north central Africa, and the Arabian Desert, which occupies most of the Arabian Peninsula, forced many people to adopt a nomadic or semi-nomadic lifestyle. For thousands of years, Bedouins herded camels, sheep and goats, traveling from region to region, adapting to the intermittent and seasonal availability of water and pasture. After the 1950's, the discovery of huge amounts of oil throughout the Middle East, and the shrinking of traditional grazing lands has shifted this pattern. Today most people live in densely populated cities. While the agricultural production of the Nile, Tigris and Euphrates valleys once supported vast ancient empires, and still is a major source of employment, the oil industry is the source of wealth and power in the Middle East today.

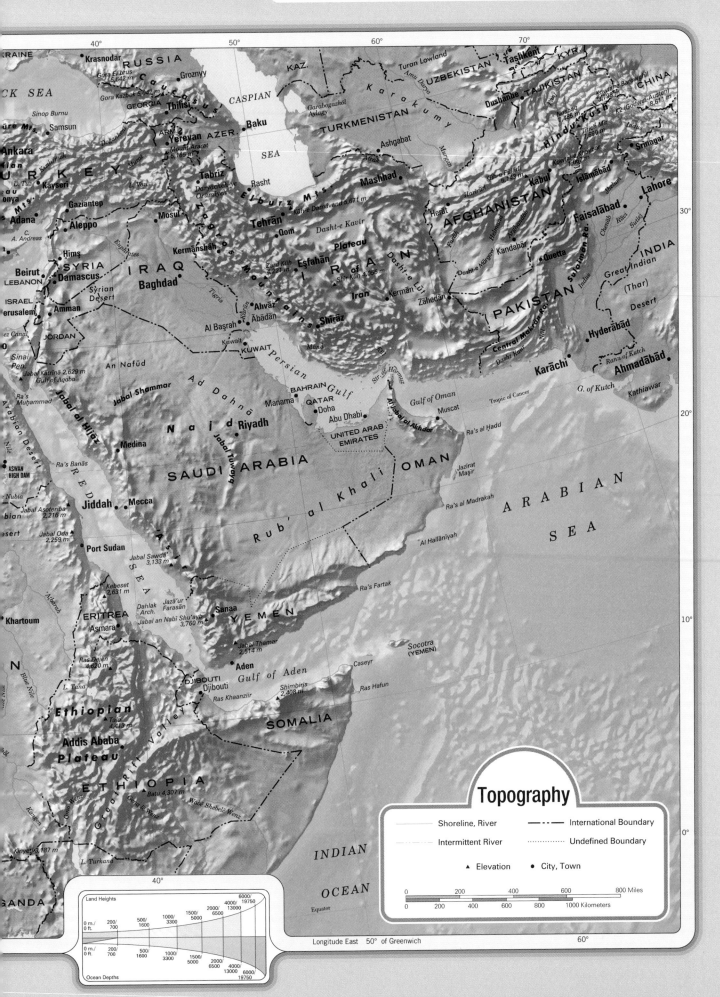

Topography

Shoreline, River	International Boundary
Intermittent River	Undefined Boundary
▲ Elevation	● City, Town

0   200   400   600   800 Miles

0   200   400   600   800   1000 Kilometers

Land Heights

6000/ 19750
4000/ 13000
2000/ 6500
1500/ 5000
1000/ 3300
500/ 1600
200/ 700
0 m./ 0 ft.

Ocean Depths

0 m./ 0 ft.
200/ 700
500/ 1600
1000/ 3300
1500/ 5000
2000/ 6500
4000/ 13000
6000/ 19750

Longitude East   50° of Greenwich   60°

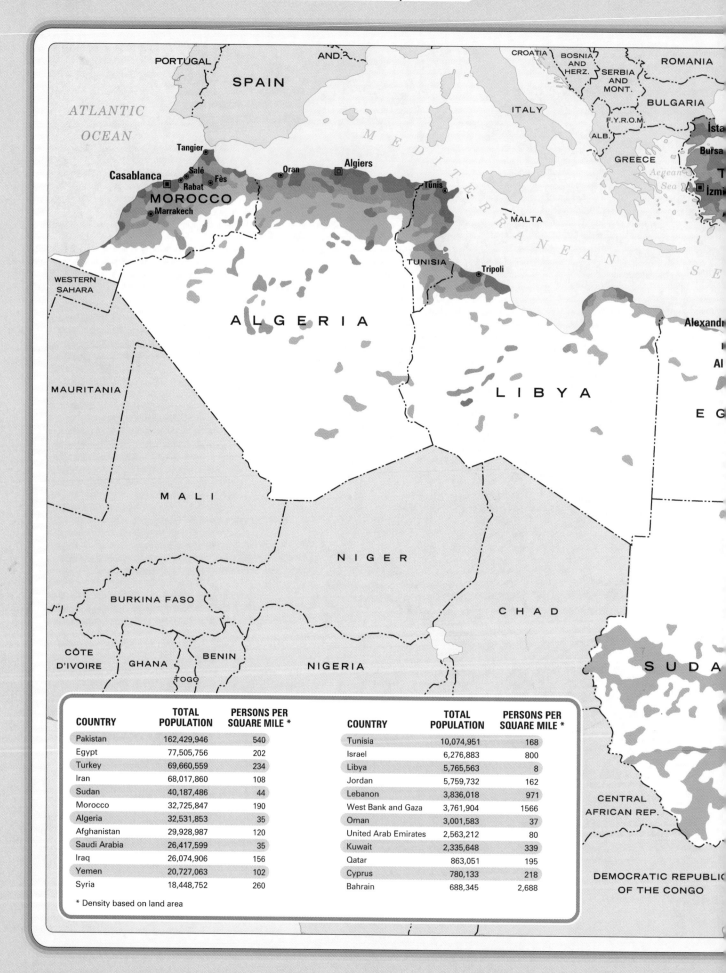

COUNTRY	TOTAL POPULATION	PERSONS PER SQUARE MILE *	COUNTRY	TOTAL POPULATION	PERSONS PER SQUARE MILE *
Pakistan	162,429,946	540	Tunisia	10,074,951	168
Egypt	77,505,756	202	Israel	6,276,883	800
Turkey	69,660,559	234	Libya	5,765,563	8
Iran	68,017,860	108	Jordan	5,759,732	162
Sudan	40,187,486	44	Lebanon	3,836,018	971
Morocco	32,725,847	190	West Bank and Gaza	3,761,904	1566
Algeria	32,531,853	35	Oman	3,001,583	37
Afghanistan	29,928,987	120	United Arab Emirates	2,563,212	80
Saudi Arabia	26,417,599	35	Kuwait	2,335,648	339
Iraq	26,074,906	156	Qatar	863,051	195
Yemen	20,727,063	102	Cyprus	780,133	218
Syria	18,448,752	260	Bahrain	688,345	2,688

* Density based on land area

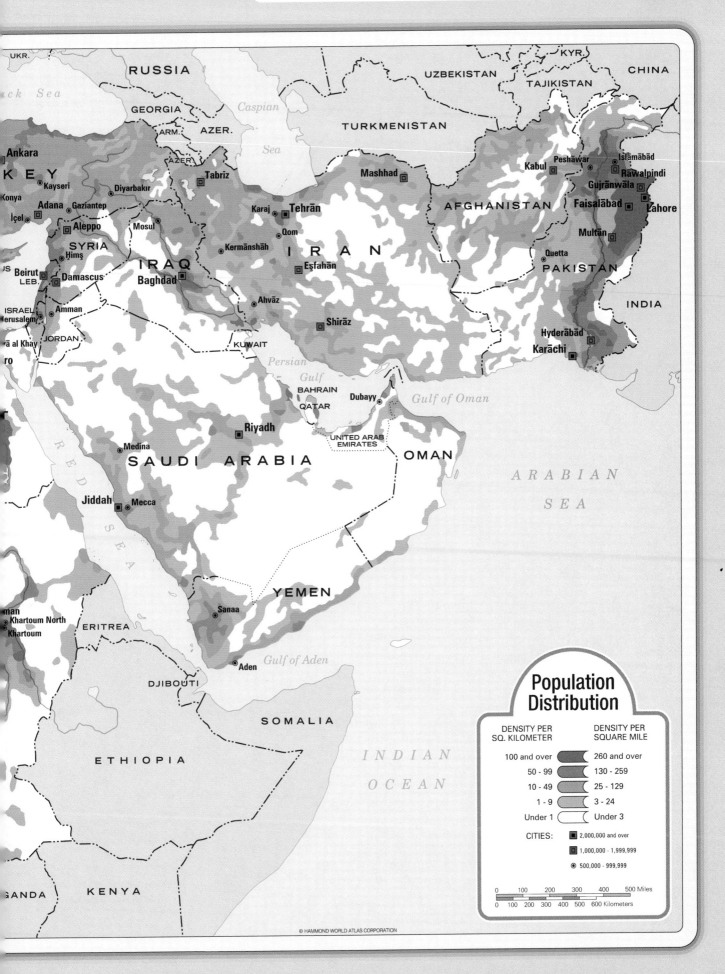

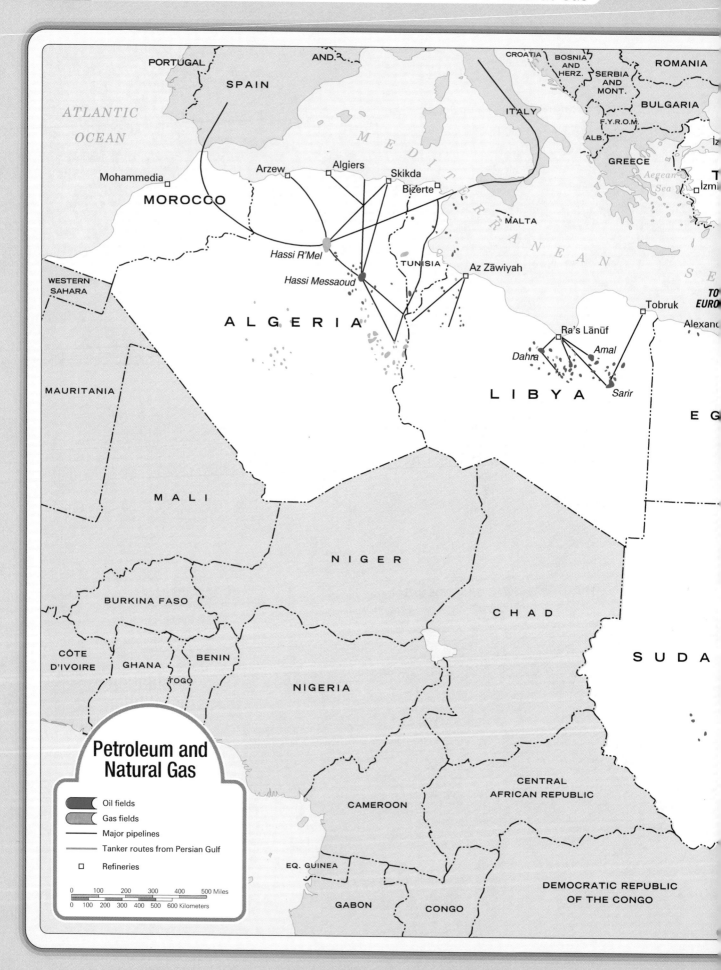

PORTUGAL
SPAIN
AND.
CROATIA
BOSNIA AND HERZ.
SERBIA AND MONT.
ROMANIA
BULGARIA
ATLANTIC OCEAN
ITALY
F.Y.R.O.M.
ALB.
GREECE
Aegean Sea
Izm
Iz
MEDITERRANEAN SEA
Mohammedia
MOROCCO
Arzew
Algiers
Skikda
Bizerte
MALTA
Hassi R'Mel
Hassi Messaoud
TUNISIA
Az Zāwiyah
TO EURO
Tobruk
Alexand
WESTERN SAHARA
ALGERIA
Ra's Lānūf
Amal
Dahra
LIBYA
Sarir
E
MAURITANIA
MALI
NIGER
CHAD
SUDA
BURKINA FASO
CÔTE D'IVOIRE
GHANA
BENIN
TOGO
NIGERIA
CAMEROON
CENTRAL AFRICAN REPUBLIC
EQ. GUINEA
GABON
CONGO
DEMOCRATIC REPUBLIC OF THE CONGO

Petroleum and Natural Gas

- Oil fields
- Gas fields
- Major pipelines
- Tanker routes from Persian Gulf
- □ Refineries

0 100 200 300 400 500 Miles
0 100 200 300 400 500 600 Kilometers

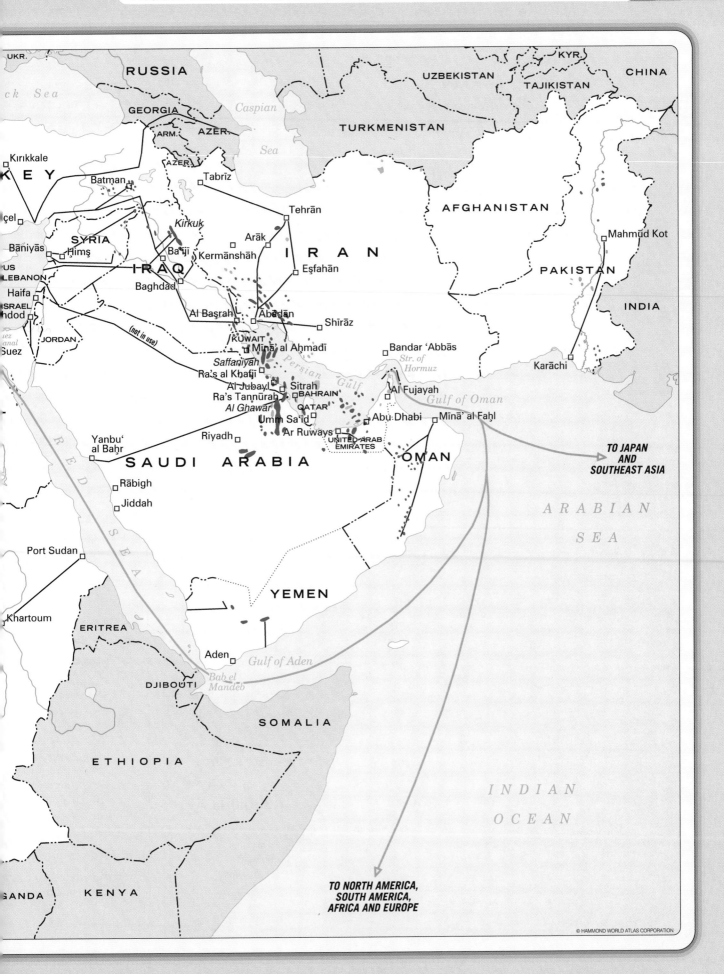

RUSSIA

UKR.

Black Sea

GEORGIA

Caspian Sea

ARM.
AZER.

AZER.

UZBEKISTAN

TAJIKISTAN

KYR.

CHINA

TURKMENISTAN

Kırıkkale

KEY

Batman

İçel

Tabrīz

Tehrān

AFGHANISTAN

SYRIA
Bāniyās
Hims

Kirkuk

Arāk

IRAN

PAKISTAN

Mahmūd Kot

US
LEBANON

Bā'jī
Kermānshāh

Esfahān

INDIA

IRAQ

Haifa

Baghdād

ISRAEL
hdod

Al Başrah

Ābādān

Shīrāz

Karāchi

JORDAN

uez
anal
Suez

(not in use)

Bandar 'Abbās

Str. of
Hormuz

Persian Gulf

KUWAIT
Mīnā' al Ahmadī

Saffānīyah
Ra's al Khafjī
Al Jubayl
Ra's Tannūrah
Al Ghawār
Umm Sa'īd

Sitrah
BAHRAIN
QATAR

Ar Ruways

Al Fujayah

Gulf of Oman

Abu Dhabi
Mīnā' al Faḥl

TO JAPAN
AND
SOUTHEAST ASIA

Yanbu'
al Bahr

Riyadh

UNITED ARAB
EMIRATES

OMAN

ARABIAN

SEA

SAUDI   ARABIA

RED SEA

Rābigh

Jiddah

Port Sudan

YEMEN

INDIAN

Khartoum

ERITREA

Aden

Gulf of Aden

OCEAN

DJIBOUTI

Bab el
Mandeb

ETHIOPIA

SOMALIA

GANDA

KENYA

TO NORTH AMERICA,
SOUTH AMERICA,
AFRICA AND EUROPE

© HAMMOND WORLD ATLAS CORPORATION

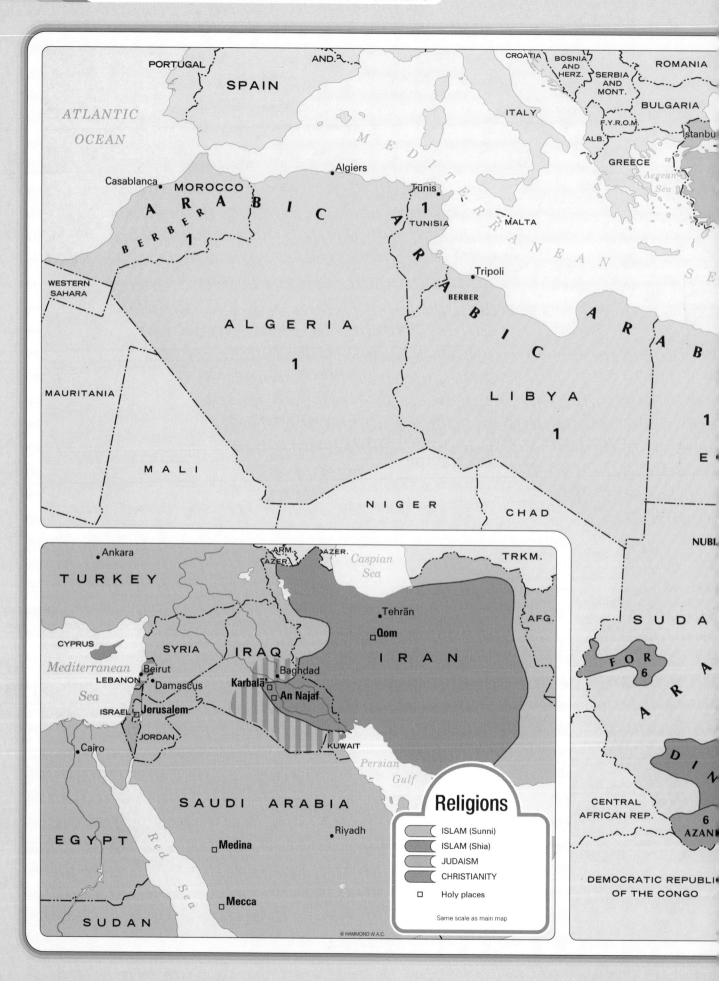

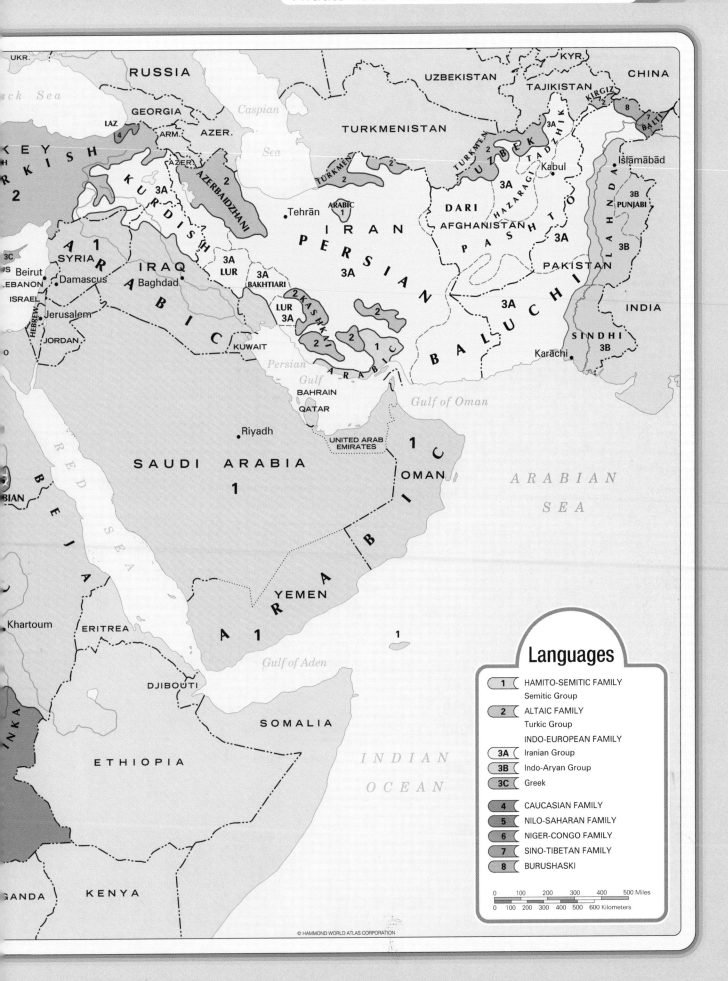

Languages

1	**HAMITO-SEMITIC FAMILY** Semitic Group
2	**ALTAIC FAMILY** Turkic Group
	INDO-EUROPEAN FAMILY
3A	Iranian Group
3B	Indo-Aryan Group
3C	Greek
4	**CAUCASIAN FAMILY**
5	**NILO-SAHARAN FAMILY**
6	**NIGER-CONGO FAMILY**
7	**SINO-TIBETAN FAMILY**
8	**BURUSHASKI**

0   100   200   300   400   500 Miles
0 100 200 300 400 500 600 Kilometers

© HAMMOND WORLD ATLAS CORPORATION

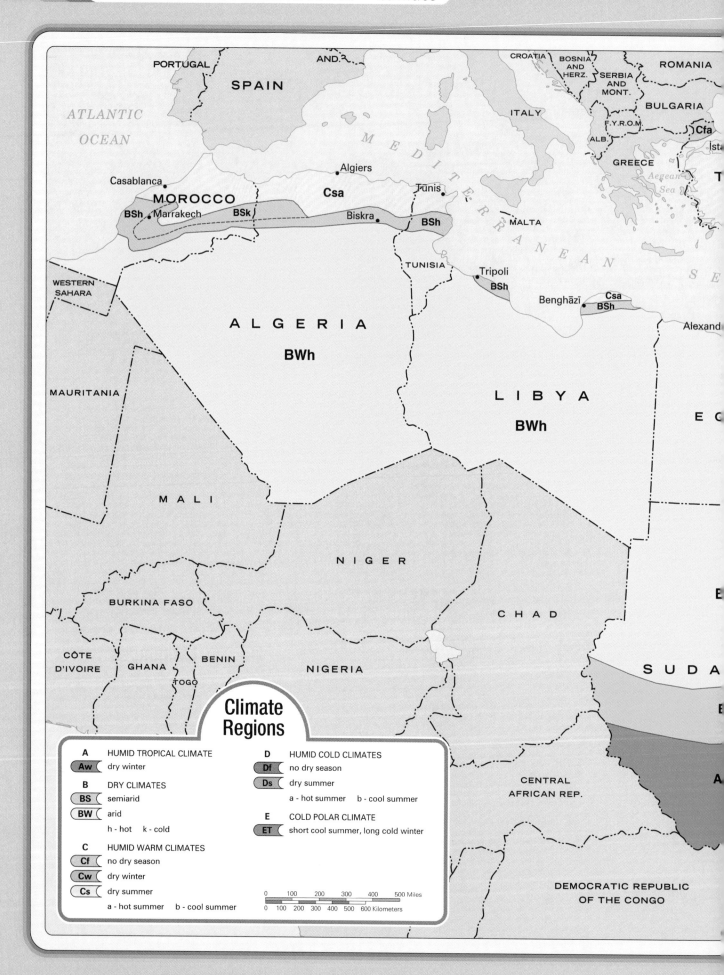

PORTUGAL

AND.

SPAIN

ATLANTIC
OCEAN

CROATIA

BOSNIA
AND
HERZ.

SERBIA
AND
MONT.

ROMANIA

BULGARIA

ITALY

F.Y.R.O.M.

ALB.

GREECE

Cfa

Ist

T

Algiers

Casablanca

MOROCCO

BSh   Marrakech

BSk

Csa

Biskra

BSh

M E D I T E R R A N E A N   S E

Tunis

MALTA

Aegean
Sea

WESTERN
SAHARA

TUNISIA

TUNISIA

Tripoli

BSh

Benghāzī

Csa

BSh

Alexand

MAURITANIA

A L G E R I A

BWh

L I B Y A

BWh

E G

MALI

N I G E R

CHAD

SUDA

BURKINA FASO

CÔTE
D'IVOIRE

GHANA

TOGO

BENIN

NIGERIA

CENTRAL
AFRICAN REP.

A

E

Climate Regions

A	HUMID TROPICAL CLIMATE		D	HUMID COLD CLIMATES
Aw	dry winter		Df	no dry season
B	DRY CLIMATES		Ds	dry summer
BS	semiarid			a - hot summer b - cool summer
BW	arid		E	COLD POLAR CLIMATE
	h - hot k - cold		ET	short cool summer, long cold winter
C	HUMID WARM CLIMATES			
Cf	no dry season			
Cw	dry winter			
Cs	dry summer			
	a - hot summer b - cool summer			

DEMOCRATIC REPUBLIC
OF THE CONGO

0   100   200   300   400   500 Miles

0   100 200 300 400 500 600 Kilometers

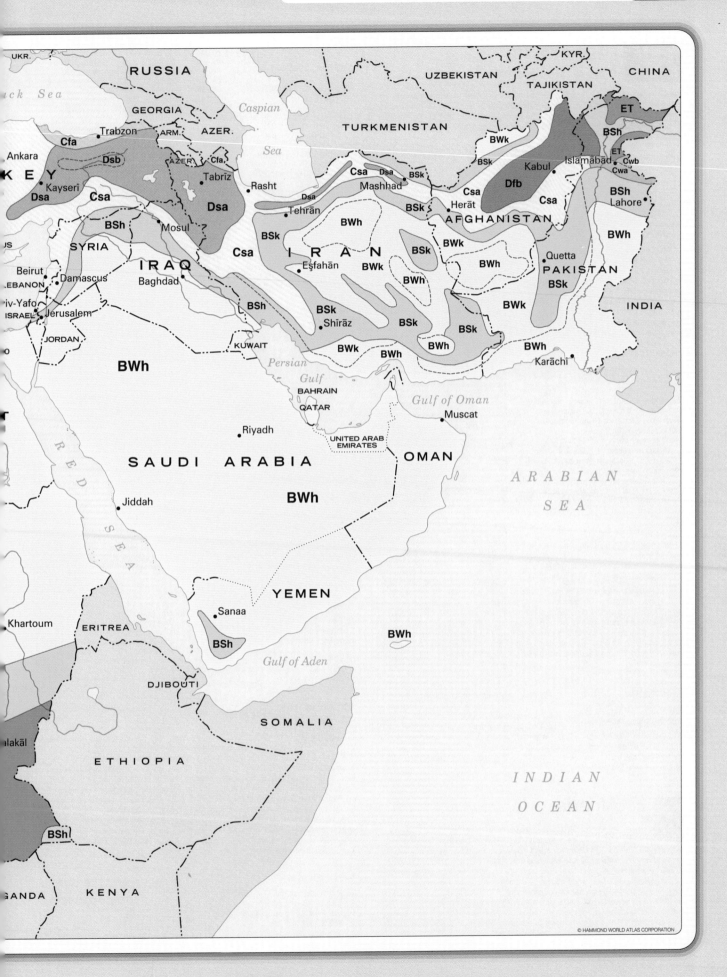

Afghanistan

Afghanistan gained independence from the United Kingdom (U.K.) in 1919. Invasion by the Soviet Union in 1979 provoked a decade-long resistance by anti-Communist rebels. After Soviet withdrawal, and the eventual collapse of the Communist regime, the Taliban seized the capital in 1996. They gained control of the country with the exception of areas held by the Northern Alliance. After the September 11th attacks on the United States, the combined U.S., Allied and Northern Alliance forces ousted the Taliban for sheltering Osama Bin Laden and other terrorists. The upheaval caused by this military intervention has been somewhat alleviated by political reconstruction and an infusion of international aid.

Geography

Total area: 250,001 sq. mi.
  (647,500 sq. km.)
Highest point: Nowshāk 24,557 ft.
  (7,485 m.)

Afghanistan's most prominent topographical features are its mountains. Parallel ranges of the Hindu Kush rise to some of the highest elevations in the world, and create deep, stream-fed valleys. These mountains also contribute to a range of climate zones, from the hot arid plains of the southwest, to the cold, wet mountains north and west of Kabul. Vegetation is largely sparse, but lush forests grow on the slopes of mountains near the border of Pakistan. Afghanistan's deep valleys provide strips of fertile, irrigated land where grain and other crops are cultivated, including fruits, nuts, wheat and corn. Afghanistan also has reserves of natural gas, petroleum, coal, copper and precious metals, but the country's daunting topography limits the development of these economic resources. In the southwest and the north, mountains finally give way to high, flat desert plains. The population is densest around the capital. Cities such as Kandahār and Baghlān seem isolated because of the rugged topography separating them from Kabul. Geographic isolation gives the regions farthest from the capital a measure of autonomy.

People

Population: 29,928,987 **Growth rate:** 4.8%
Birth rate: 47.0 births/1,000 population
Death rate: 20.8 deaths/1,000 population
Life expectancy: 42.9 years
Ethnic groups: Pashtun 42%, Tajik 27%,
  Hazara 9%, Uzbek 9%, Aimak 4%,
  Turkmen, Baloch and other 9%
Religions: Sunni Muslim 80%,
  Shi'a Muslim 19%, other 1%
Languages: Dari (Afghan Persian) 50%,
  Pashtu 35%, Turkic languages 11%

Although almost entirely Muslim, Afghanis comprise a diverse mix of people from both Persian and Turkish backgrounds. There are two official languages, Dari and Pashtun, though a mix of languages is spoken. Many Afghanis are bilingual, but few are literate. Fierce tribal and ethnic loyalties have contributed to tensions over the years, but make Afghanistan a truly polyglot state.

Government

Government type: Islamic republic
Capital: Kabul
Admin. divisions: 34 provinces (velayat)
Independence: August 19, 1919 (from U.K.)

After the collapse of the Taliban regime in 2001, a constitution was adopted setting up a bicameral legislature. The upper House of Elders is partly elected by provisional and district councils, and partly appointed by the president. The lower House of the People is directly elected in proportion to the population of each province. A new president, Hamid Karzai, was elected in October, 2004. The constitution states that no law should be contrary to Islam. Also the state is obliged to create a society based on social justice, protection of human rights, democracy, and to ensure national unity and equality between all ethnic groups and tribes. This mandate will be difficult to achieve, but growing political stability and continued international attention make Afghanistan's future outlook more promising.

Economy

GDP- real growth rate: 7.5%
GDP- per capita: $800
Currency: afghani (AFN)

Afghanistan's traditional economy of nomadic sheep herding, subsistence farming and traditional handcrafts has been seriously disrupted by political upheavals, and its people remain poor. Desperate farmers have been turning to illegal crops, such as opium, which can be readily turned into cash. Major challenges facing the new government are the alleviation of housing and water shortages and a lack of medical care and jobs.

Algeria

Its name was derived from the Arabic word for "islands" (al-jazair) in observance of the islets in the harbor at Algiers. The Arab invasions of the 8th and 11th Centuries A.D. brought Islam and the Arabic language to North Africa. The influx of people and ideas from Africa, Asia and Europe (particularly France) bestowed Algeria with a diverse ethnic and cultural mix that now challenges its progression from third-world country to modern nation. The borders of modern Algeria were created by the French colonization of 1830. Though independence came in 1962, the final yokes of French colonialism were decades in being released. The subsequent years as an independent nation saw violence, upheaval and a whipsawed economy. The country's petroleum resources have yet to be sufficiently exploited to redress Algeria's social and economic challenges.

Geography

Total area: 919,595 sq. mi.
  (2,381,740 sq. km.)
Highest point: Tahat 9,851 ft.
  (3,003 m.)

Algeria, the second largest country in Africa, extends deep into the Sahara Desert. Algeria's cities and population are concentrated along the narrow, northern coastal plain, while most of the country's mineral riches are found in the remote, arid areas of the south. From the coast, the land rises as the Tell, a fertile, sometimes mountainous region with verdant valleys separating the coast from the interior high plains. Southward, the Hauts Plateaux, a vast arid plain, broken by occasional ridges and salt lakes (chotts), lies between the Tell Atlas and the Saharan Atlas mountains. Descending the vast Saharan expanse, the landscape becomes an inhospitable desert, dotted by occasional fertile oases. Approaching the Niger frontier, the land again uplifts forming the Ahaggar highlands, home of Algeria's highest point, Tahat.

The northern Algerian coast benefits from a Mediterranean climate with cool, wet winters and hot dry summers. The coastal Tell and eastern mountains receive the most precipitation, falling from September into the early winter. In the high plateau areas, the winters become increasingly colder and drier. Blowing in from the desert to the south, the hot, dusty, sand-laden wind (the sirocco) intermittently penetrates these otherwise moderate climates. The vast Sahara desert region of the south experiences blistering heat and chilly nights resulting in extreme daily temperature ranges.

Camel caravan, Algeria

People

Population: 32,531,853
Population growth rate: 1.22%
Birth rate: 17.13 births/1,000 population
Death rate: 4.6 deaths/1,000 population
Life expectancy: 73 years
Ethnic groups: Arab-Berber 99%, European
  less than 1%
Religions: Sunni Muslim (state religion) 99%,
  Christian and Jewish 1%
Languages: Arabic (official), French,
  Berber dialects

Most Algerians consider themselves Arab but are Berber in origin. Those who identify themselves as Berber rather than Arab live mostly in the mountainous region of Kabylie, east of Algiers. These people identify with their Berber rather than their Arab cultural heritage. Neglected by the government, the Berbers have long agitated for more autonomy. Despite the government direction towards Arabization since independence, Algerian culture remains both a complementary and contentious mix of Berber, French and Arab influences.

Government

Government type: republic
Capital: Algiers
Admin. divisions: 48 provinces (wilayas)
Independence: July 5, 1962 (from France)

The post-independence socialist government focused their attention on Arabization and the escape from French colonial influence. In the 1980's, economic stagnation and a rising Islamic movement led to a decade of violence which, in 1999, was somewhat tempered by an amnesty program for the rebels. In 2001, a Berber uprising resulted in the recognition of their language, Tamazight, as a national, if not official, language. Violence gradually abated and the elections of 2004 were deemed to be the fairest seen in Algeria.

Economy

GDP- real growth rate: 6.1%
GDP- per capita: $6,000
Currency: Algerian dinar (DZD)

Hydrocarbons form the backbone of the Algerian economy, comprising 95% of the country's exports. Diversification of the economy has been slow, and export revenues must often be used to purchase capital goods and food. Citrus, olives and dates are important agricultural products. Although much diminished from its importance in the colonial economy, in a country whose religion forbids the consumption of alcohol, wine remains an important commercial product.

Bahrain

The name Bahrain means "Two Seas," referring to the two water sources on the island, freshwater springs and the salty surrounding sea. Historically, its strategic position has attracted several invaders: Assyrians, Babylonians, Greeks, Persians, and finally Arabs who gave the country its Muslim culture. Originally, Bahrain comprised the eastern province of what is now Saudi Arabia as well as the offshore island of Awal, until the Portuguese separated these regions in 1521. The modern state of Bahrain derives from British support of the Al-Khalifa family in order to liberate the island from Iran in 1869. Though Bahrain gained independence from the U.K. in 1971, Iran has periodically asserted claim to Bahrain. Rich petroleum reserves have made this tiny island nation wealthy, but require Bahrain to play a delicate foreign policy balancing act. To offset its dependence on oil, Bahrain has strived to become an international center of finance and trade.

Geography

Total area: 257 sq. mi.
  (665 sq. km.)
Highest point: Jabal ad Dukhan
  400 ft. (122 m.)

Bahrain is an island nation in the Persian Gulf archipelago, connected to Saudi Arabia by the King Fahd Causeway, one of the longest bridges in the world. The island consists of a low desert plain rising gently to a central ridge. The arid climate features mild winters and hot, humid summers. The lack of fertile soil and sufficient land area has severely limited agriculture.

Although shrimp, fish and pearls are found off the coast, agriculture contributes less than one percent to the Gross Domestic Product (GDP). The country makes its money from petroleum products, shipping and banking.

People

Population: 688,345 **Growth rate:** 1.5%
Birth rate: 18.1 births/1,000 population
Death rate: 4.1 deaths/1,000 population
Life expectancy: 74 years
Ethnic groups: Bahraini 63%, Asian 19%, other Arab 10%, Iranian 8%
Religions: Shi'a Muslim 70%, Sunni Muslim 30%
Languages: Arabic, (official), English, Farsi, Urdu

Bahrain has developed a highly international economy. Foreign-born residents and workers come largely from Asian and other Arab countries, and the several different languages spoken reflect this diverse community. The country is noted for its freedom of speech. Its highly urbanized population lives in an area only 3.5 times the size of Washington, D.C., giving it the highest population density of any Middle Eastern country. Street life in Manama is highly cosmopolitan. Paradoxically, the traditional Bahraini ways of cloth weaving, pottery making and building traditional fishing boats (dhows) are still evident, even in the cities.

Government

Government type: constitutional monarchy
Capital: Manama
Admin. divisions: 5 governorates
Independence: August 15, 1971 (from U.K.)

The Al-Khalifa family has ruled Bahrain since 1783. The government has pushed economic and political reform, given women the right to vote, and worked to improve relations with the majority Shi'a community. Changes in the constitution providing for a partially elected legislature and an independent judicial system were approved by Bahraini voters.

Economy

GDP- real growth rate: 5.6%
GDP- per capita: $19,200
Currency: Bahraini dinar (BHD)

Petroleum production and refining account for 60% of Bahrain's exports and 30% of its GDP. Services, dominated by banking, account for 58% of the GDP. Other industries include aluminum and textiles. A vibrant service sector and construction projects, (including a causeway to Qatar), assure continued economic growth as oil reserves become depleted.

Cyprus

Located in the northeast corner of the Mediterranean, Cyprus has historically been a stopping point on trade routes between the Middle East and Western Europe. It was part of the Ottoman Empire from 1570 to 1878, when the Cyprus Convention ceded Cyprus to Great Britain for its support of the Ottomans in the Russian-Turkish war. Cyprus was controlled by the U.K. until 1960. Tensions between Greek and Turkish Cypriots came to a head in 1963, when Turkish Cypriots withdrew from the government, and violence broke out in Nicosia. Sporadic violence has continued since. A Greek-supported coup attempt in 1974 resulted in the Greek Cypriot government controlling the southwest two thirds of the island and Turkish Cypriots controlling the northeast third. The U.K. retains title to two military bases on the southern coast. A United Nations (U.N.) monitored buffer zone runs through the center of Nicosia dividing the two sides.

Geography

Total area: 3,571 sq. mi. (9,250 sq. km.)
Highest point: Mount Olympus 6,401 ft. (1,951 m.)

Cyprus has two parallel mountain ranges running east to west, separated by a high central plain. Surrounding the island are sporadic coastal plains. Its climate is temperate, with hot, dry summers, and cool, rainy winters. Its scenic topography attracts tourists from around the world. Though the capital is located in the north central section of the island, the other major cities are situated on the coast.

People

Population: 780,133 **Growth rate:** 0.6%
Birth rate: 17.1 births/1,000 population
Death rate: 7.6 deaths/1,000 population
Life expectancy: 78 years
Ethnic groups: Greek 77%, Turkish 18%, other 5%
Religions: Greek Orthodox 77%, Muslim 18%, other 4%
Languages: Greek, Turkish, English

As a result of the expulsion of Greek Cypriots from the north, and Turkish Cypriots fleeing the south after the 1974 division of the island, southern Cyprus is predominantly Greek, while the northern part is mostly Turkish. Historically, the two ethnic groups were evenly distributed throughout the island, though Greek settlers have always been more numerous. Greek and Turkish Cypriots have many customs in common, but maintain their ethnicity by their religion, language, and political ties.

Government

Government type: republic
Capital: Nicosia
Admin. divisions: 6 districts (Greek area)
Independence: August 16, 1960 (from U.K.)

The 1960 constitution set up a system of government with intricate checks and balances, and a power sharing ratio designed to protect the interests of Turkish Cypriots. The executive branch was to be headed by a Greek Cypriot president, and a Turkish Cypriot Vice President, each possessing a veto over certain types of legislation. This arrangement failed to prevent escalating tension between the two sides. Following independence, Greek Cypriots voted three times to merge with Greece, but Greece did not pursue this course. In 1974, the military junta in control of

Greece decided to sponsor a coup in Nicosia to bring about unification. Fearing for the rights of the Turkish minority, Turkey invaded Cyprus, capturing the northern third of the island. In 1983, Turkish Cypriots proclaimed a separate state under Rauf Denktash, called the "Turkish Republic of Northern Cyprus." Despite failed reunification with the north, Southern Cyprus joined the E.U. in 2004 as a divided state. In 2005, the election of Mehmet Ali Talat as Denktash's successor led to renewed discussion of reunification, but the two sides were unable to come to an agreement.

Economy

GDP- real growth rate: Greek area: 3.2%, Turkish area: 2.6%
GDP- per capita:
Greek area: $20,300
Turkish area: $7,135
Currency:
Greek area: Cypriot pound (CYP)
Turkish area: Turkish Lira (TRL)

In addition to its copper, Cyprus is known for its agricultural exports, such as citrus, grapes, olives, lamb and dairy products. Other exports include pharmaceuticals, cement and clothing. The Greek Cypriot economy is prosperous, but its erratic growth rate reflects the fact that tourism fluctuates greatly with the political instability in the region. The Turkish sector is also volatile and is hampered by its reliance on a weaker Turkish currency. Since the Turkish Republic is only recognized by Turkey, it is difficult for the north to establish trade relations and foreign financing.

Egypt

Egypt became one of the world's great civilizations partly because of the regularity and richness of the annual Nile River flood, and partly because the surrounding desert lands afforded a degree of protection from invasion. From 3200 B.C. to 343 B.C., Egypt was ruled by native dynasties. Free from foreign control, Egyptian Pharohs produced some of the world's most stunning ancient monuments, including the pyramids at Giza, the temple at Karnak and the tombs in the Valley of the Kings. Once these kingdoms weakened, Persian rule was followed by Greek, Roman, and Byzantine rule, but it was the Arabs who introduced their language and religion in the seventh century A.D., and gave rise to the culture we see in Egypt today. The Mamluks, a local military caste took control about 1250, and continued to be the ruling caste after the conquest of Egypt by the Ottoman Turks in 1517. After the completion of the Suez Canal made Egypt an international transportation hub but left the government in debt, Great Britain seized control in 1882, ostensibly to protect its investments. Partially independent from the U.K. in 1922, Egypt gained full sovereignty after World War II.

Sphinx and Chephren Pyramid, Egypt

Geography

Total area: 386,662 sq. mi. (1,001,450 sq. km.)
Highest point: Jabal Kātrinā 8,625 ft. (2,629 m.)

The Nile is the source of Egypt's wealth and culture. The extraordinarily fertile floodplain and delta afforded a dependable base for cultivation of food crops in an otherwise barren and arid land. Its vast desert plateau is dotted with occasional oases and crossed by the Nile delta and floodplain. The completion of the Aswan High Dam in 1970 controlled the annual flood and made Egyptian agriculture almost entirely dependent on irrigation. Today, the vast majority of Egypt's population still lives within a mile or two of the banks of the Nile. Egypt is the most populous Arab country, and occupies a geographically strategic position as gateway between the Mediterranean Sea and the Indian Ocean via the Suez Canal and the Red Sea. Politically, its historic position as the cultural center of the Islamic world has made Egypt an important international mediator, helping to resolve disputes among various Arab nations. The capital, Cairo, is the largest city in Africa, and one of the most populous cities in the world.

People

Population: 77,505,756 **Growth rate:** 1.8%
Birth rate: 23.3 births/1,000 population
Death rate: 5.3 deaths/1,000 population
Life expectancy: 71 years
Ethnic groups: Eastern Hamitic 99%, other 1%
Religions: Muslim 94%, Coptic Christian and other 6%
Languages: Arabic (official), English and French

Egyptians are a fairly homogenous ethnic group, and retain strong genetic ties to their ancient forebears, although no conclusive theory has been offered explaining their origins. Ethnic minorities include a small group of Bedouin Arab nomads who live in the eastern and western desert areas, and Nubians who live along the Nile in southern Egypt. The dominant economic position of Cairo and Alexandria, combined with the concentration of the population along the Nile make modern Egypt a largely urban society.

Government

Government type: republic
Capital: Cairo
Admin. divisions: 26 governorates
Independence: February 28, 1922 (from U.K.)

Egypt's government is theoretically a multiparty system with parliamentary elections, and with executive power divided between the president and prime minister. In practice, President Mubarak has been the only candidate for president, and his party has also filled the post of Prime Minister since the assassination of Anwar Sadat in 1981. Recently Mubarak has announced the reform of election law, paving the way for multi-candidate voting for the first time in Egypt's history. Its legal system is based on a mix of English common law, Islamic law and Napoleonic codes. Egypt was the first Arab country to establish peace with Israel, signing the Israel Peace Treaty after the Camp David Accords in 1979.

Economy

GDP- real growth rate: 4.5%
GDP- per capita: $4,200
Currency: Egyptian pound (EGP)

Though Egypt is no longer dependent on the Nile's annual flood to fertilize its fields, the country's destiny is still closely tied to the Nile. Rising population and pollution threatens Egypt's water supply, and strains its agricultural production. Egypt is the third largest recipient of foreign aid from the U.S. following the Iraq war. Egypt also exports petroleum, natural gas, iron ore and other natural resources, and has recently adopted measures to increase foreign investment. Egypt's merchant marine is second only to Turkey among Middle East nations. Tourism gives a major boost to its economy. Egypt also boasts a thriving media and movie industry.

Iran

Formerly known as Persia in the west, the country has been called Iran by its people since ancient times. After the ruling monarchy was overthrown and the shah was forced into exile, the country became an Islamic republic in 1979. Conservative clerics ultimately established a theocratic system of government. U.S.-Iranian relations have been strained since a group of Iranian students seized the U.S. Embassy in Tehrän on November 4, 1979, and held hostages there for 444 days. From 1980-1988, Iran fought a bloody, inconclusive war with Iraq that eventually led to clashes with the U.S. Navy in the Persian Gulf during 1987 and 1988. Recent efforts at political reform have been resisted by entrenched conservative politicians, aided by the Supreme Leader who has wide veto power over parliamentary reforms judged to be contrary to Islamic law. Iran has been sanctioned by the U.S. for sponsoring terrorism in Lebanon and elsewhere.

Tomb of Moshtag Ali Shah, Iran

Geography

Total area: 636,296 sq. mi.
  (1,648,000 sq. km.)
Highest point: Küh-e Damävand
  18,605 ft. (5,671 m.)

Iran has some discontinuous coastal plains, but is dominated by mountain ranges separating various plateaus, and surrounds a high central basin. On the Caspian coastal plain, temperatures are subtropical, and the area is humid and wet. At higher elevations in the western part of the country, winters can be severe, and snowfall can be heavy. The eastern and central basins are arid, sometimes desert lands dotted with salt lakes, and the southern coastal plains feature mild winters and humid, hot summers.

People

Population: 68,017,860 **Growth rate:** 0.9%
Birth rate: 16.8 births/1,000 population
Death rate: 5.6 deaths/1,000 population
Life expectancy: 70 years
Ethnic groups: Persian 51%, Azeri 24%, Gilaki and Mazandarani 8%, Kurd 7%, other 10%
Religions: Shi'a Muslim 89%, Sunni Muslim 9%, Zoroastrian, Jewish, Christian and Baha'i 2%
Languages: Persian, Turkic, Kurdish and others

Almost two-thirds of Iran's people are of Aryan origin whose ancestors migrated from Central Asia. Iran's nearly 80 diverse ethnic groups include Persians, Kurds, Lurs and Baluchi. They are held together by a common sense of their rich culture and history. Throughout recorded history, Persian art, music, architecture, poetry and philosophy have made important contributions to the global community, and are a continued source of national pride.

Government

Government type: Islamic republic
Capital: Tehrän
Admin. divisions: more than 30 provinces (in transition)
Independence: April 1, 1979

The former Shah of Iran was strongly supported by British and American interests. In 1953, the removal of powerful and popular Prime Minister Mohammed Mosaddeq, orchestrated by U.K. and U.S. intelligence agencies, helped consolidate the shah's hold on power. He modernized the oil industry but crushed civil liberties. His autocratic rule led to the Iranian Revolution and the overthrow of his regime in 1979. An Islamic republic under Ayatollah Khomeni was established by popular vote. The government has often pursued anti-Western policies. More recently, economic reforms to diversify Iran's oil-dependent economy have been more successful than political reforms aimed at liberalizing the Iranian state. Conservative forces are aided by an intricate governmental structure that privileges Islamic law and resists Parliamentary reforms.

Economy

GDP- real growth rate: 6.3%
GDP- per capita: $7,700
Currency: Iranian rial (IRR)

Iran is the Organization of Petroleum Exporting Countries (OPEC) second largest producer of oil, and also has large reserves of natural gas. Showing increased independence from OPEC, Iran plans to participate in a new International Oil Bourse, trading oil priced differently than in other markets, in an effort to rebalance trading relationships. Though Iran's large industries are mostly state-controlled, small scale private industries are part of the mix. State investment in agriculture and irrigation has modernized production techniques and opened new markets for Iranian produce. Iran is also interested in encouraging a favorable climate for foreign investors to help diversify their economy. Budget deficits remain a problem, even in years of high prices for oil, because of large state subsidies to certain parts of the economy.

Iraq

★✓★☆★

Iraq was historically part of Mesopotamia, meaning "land between the rivers." It is located at the confluence of the Tigris and Euphrates, and was the cradle of the Sumerian, Akkadian, Babylonian, and Assyrian civilizations. It was regarded as the anchor of the Fertile Crescent, an area stretching from Palestine to the Persian Gulf. Formerly a part of the Ottoman Empire, Iraq was occupied by Great Britain during World War I, and gained independence as a kingdom in 1932. A republic was proclaimed in 1958, but a series of military strongmen, ending with Saddam Hussein in 1979, ruled Iraq. Years of turmoil and ethnic strife followed, including a bloody Iran-Iraq war from 1980-1988 which ended in a stalemate. In 1991, Iraq's invasion of Kuwait prompted a U.S.-led U.N. coalition to liberate Kuwait, and sanction the Hussein regime. Hussein's continued disregard of U.N. authority led to his removal by international forces in 2003. Currently, the Iraqi Interim Government is drafting a new constitution which provides for Iraq's future governance.

Geography

Total area: 168,754 sq. mi.
  (437,072 sq. km.)
Highest point: unnamed peak
  11,847 ft. (3,611 m.)

Iraq is dominated by a large central desert plain, which gives way to marshes in the south and mountains in the north. Irrigated lands along and between the Tigris and Euphrates supplement agricultural production. Marshy areas near the Shatt al-Arab, Iraq's strategic waterway to the Persian Gulf, have been largely drained by government water control projects. A hot, dry desert climate with mild winters and hot, cloudless summers predominates. Northern mountainous regions see cold winters with heavy snowfalls, which cause flooding downstream during the spring thaw. Iraq's frequent sandstorms are caused by strong winds picking up sand and loose soil. At certain times of the year, the hot desert air causes the lower atmosphere to become unstable, and makes winds at the surface become even more violent. This creates almost a cyclonic wall of sand with clear, blue sky above the center of the storm.

People

Population: 26,074,906 **Growth rate:** 2.7%
Birth rate: 32.5 births/1,000 population
Death rate: 5.5 deaths/1,000 population
Life expectancy: 69 years
Ethnic groups: Arab 75-80%, Kurdish 15-20%, Turkoman, Assyrian or other 5%
Religions: Shi'a Muslim 60-65%, Sunni Muslim 32-37%, Christian or other 5%
Languages: Arabic, Kurdish, Assyrian, Armenian

The majority of Iraq's people are Shi'a Muslims, although Saddam Hussein's totalitarian regime favored Sunni Muslims and persecuted the Shi'a community while co-opting its wealthiest members. This favoritism fostered deep rifts separating Iraq's ethnic groups, a conflict which has erupted since the removal of Saddam's oppressive control. The regime also persecuted the Kurdish people in the northern part of the country because of their desire for autonomy. A sizeable population of Arabs inhabiting the marshy areas in the southeast has been displaced by water control projects. These projects drained much of the wetlands, threatening the livelihood of the inhabitants as well as posing a serious threat to wildlife. Healing these ethnic and economic divisions will be a major task of the new government in Iraq.

Government

Government type: in transition
Capital: Baghdad
Admin. divisions: 18 governorates (muhafazat)
Independence: October 3, 1932 (from League of Nations mandate under U.K. administration). On June 28, 2004, the Coalition Provisional Authority transferred sovereignty to the Iraqi Interim Government.

The Interim Government of Iraq is a Transitional National Assembly of 275 members. Despite continuing upheaval and a strong insurgency, it has founded institutions necessary to govern the country. It has drafted a permanent constitution which paved the way for national elections at the end of 2005. The Shia-led United Iraqi Alliance emerged as the winner, but failed to gain a full majority.

Economy

GDP- real growth rate: 52.3%
GDP- per capita: $3,500
Currency: New Iraqi Dinar (NID)

Iraq's economy is dominated by the oil sector, which has traditionally provided about 95% of foreign exchange earnings. Agricultural products include wheat, barley, rice, vegetables, dates, cotton, cattle, sheep and poultry. International sanctions following Iraq's seizure of Kuwait in 1991, and damage from subsequent military intervention, crippled the economy until the institution of the U.N.'s oil for food program in 1996. This program allowed limited exports of oil in order to pay for food and medicine. The large gain in GDP in 2004 is the result of starting from a low base in the wake of the collapse of the Hussein regime. Although comparatively little infrastructure was destroyed during hostilities, looting, insurgent attacks and sabotage hamper efforts to restart the economy.

Israel

For over 3,000 years, the region of Palestine has been regarded as a Holy Land by both Jews and Muslims, and has been subject to conflicting territorial claims. During Roman times, Jewish population dwindled after the failure of the Great Jewish Revolt. The first wave of Jewish migration back to Israel started in the late 1800's, and saw the founding of the international Zionist movement. The second wave occurred during the first two decades of the 20th century, and led to the Balfour Declaration by Great Britain favoring the establishment of a Jewish national home. By 1940, subsequent waves of emigrants increased the Jewish population in Palestine to 30% of the total. By that time, the British came to view the Balfour Declaration as unworkable, and started to implement plans for a joint Arab-Israeli state. Jerusalem was to be an international zone under U.N. administration, but these plans were not fully implemented due to World War II. Increasing levels of violence by militant groups led the U.K. to withdraw from Palestine in 1948. The U.N.

partitioned the area into Arab and Jewish states, but this arrangement was rejected by Palestinian Arabs, who subsequently launched a guerilla war. The State of Israel was proclaimed on May 14, 1948, an announcement soon greeted by the invasion of armed forces from Transjordan, Syria, and Lebanon. The 1948-1949 Arab-Israeli conflict, as well as subsequent military conflicts in 1967 and 1973, have secured the existence of the State of Israel, but have not resolved the deep mistrust between the two sides or resolved the issue of how power is to be shared in the region.

Geography

Total area: 8,019 sq. mi.
(20,770 sq. km.)
(excludes disputed areas under Israeli control)
Highest point: Har Meron
3,963 ft. (1,208 m.)

Israel's climate is hot and dry in southern and eastern desert areas, but the Mediterranean coast is more temperate. A low coastal plain rises to a central mountain chain dominated by Israel's highest peak. The land then falls sharply into the Jordan rift valley and the shores of the Dead Sea. Well below sea level, this area contains the lowest point on earth at -1,339 feet (-408 meters). Israel has occupied the West Bank and East Jerusalem in Jordan, the Golan Heights in Syria and the Gaza Strip on the border with Egypt since 1967. For additional information on the West Bank and Gaza Strip please see page 27.

Tower of David grounds, Israel

People

Population: 6,276,883 **Growth rate:** 1.2%
Birth rate: 18.2 births/1,000 population
Death rate: 6.2 deaths/1,000 population
Life expectancy: 79 years
Ethnic groups: Jewish 80.1%,
non-Jewish (mostly Arab) 19.9%
Religions: Jewish 80.1%, Muslim 14.6%
(mostly Sunni), Christian 2.1%, other 3.2%
Languages: Hebrew (official), Arabic, English

Jewish population in the region was quite small at the time the first waves of emigrants fleeing persecution arrived in Palestine in the late 1800's. Subsequent periods of immigration increased the Jewish population in the region to 30% in 1940. Within a year of independence, the immigration of Holocaust survivors and Jews from Arab lands doubled Israel's population. During the late 1980's and early 1990's, one million Jewish people from the former Soviet Union immigrated to Israel. Hebrew is the primary official language of Israel, and Arabic is the official language of the Arab minority. Though ethnically and religiously Israel is a Jewish state, it is not a theocracy, and its laws respect other traditions. Though 80% of the population is Jewish, about one half of Israeli Jews consider themselves secular in practice.

Government

Government type: parliamentary democracy
Capital: Jerusalem
Admin. divisions: 6 districts (mehozot)
Independence: May 14, 1948 (League of Nations mandate under U.K. administration)

Israel does not have a formal constitution, but is governed by the 15 Basic Laws of Israel passed by the 120-member parliament called the Knesset. These laws have a special status and will be incorporated into the official constitution currently being drafted. In criminal commercial law, Israel's legal system is a mix of English common law and British Mandate regulations, and in personal matters, a mix of Jewish, Christian, and Muslim traditions. The Israeli military is highly trained, well-equipped, and battle tested, having defended Israel in five major wars. Most Israelis, men and women, must serve a specified period in the armed forces, with the exception of Israeli Arabs and confirmed pacifists.

Economy

GDP- real growth rate: 3.9%
GDP- per capita: $20,800
Currency: new Israeli shekel (NIS)

Agriculture was an early key to Israel's survival, producing valuable cash crops for export and making Israel's food production self-sufficient with the continued exception of imported grain and beef. Irrigation systems have made desert areas bloom, but strain the region's limited supply of fresh water by cutting the flow of the Jordan River and causing the Dead Sea to retreat. Fruits, vegetables and flowers are major exports, but Israel's high-tech industries have long since eclipsed the agricultural sector in economic importance. Industrial exports include military equipment, diamonds, software, semiconductors, pharmaceuticals and chemicals. Despite a highly industrialized economy and a robust service sector, Israel runs a continuing trade deficit. The U.S. has long been a major source of economic and military aid.

Jordan

Jordan's modern history was largely shaped during the rule of King Hussein from 1953-1999. For decades after the rejected partition of Palestine led to armed conflict with Israel, Hussein had to contend with competing pressures from the three major powers with interests in the region (the U.S., U.K., and U.S.S.R.). He also had to deal with nationalist pressures from other Arab states as well as a growing Jordanian population of Palestinian refugees while weathering several coup attempts. In 1946, Transjordan, as it was then known, supported Palestinian nationalists opposed to the creation of Israel. The Jordanian military fought in the 1948 and 1967 Arab-Israeli Conflicts. But in the late 1960's, when the power of the Palestinian resistance fighters (the fedayeen) threatened Jordan's internal security, King Hussein moved to expel them with military force, and distance his government from the Palestine Liberation Organization (PLO). These moves ultimately led to a peace treaty with Israel in 1994. Based on Hussein's largely successful efforts at being a moderating force in the region, especially in the later years of his rule, Jordan continues to remain at peace with its neighbors. Following the outbreak of Israeli-Palestinian fighting in 2000 Jordan offered its help as a mediator.

Geography

Total area: 35,637 sq. mi.
(92,300 sq. km.)
Highest point: Jabal Ramm
5,689 ft. (1,734 m.)

Jordan is largely desert, but does have a rainy season in the west from November to April. Jordan's lack of natural resources such as oil, arable land and fresh water continue to affect its economy. The Great Rift Valley, comprising some of the world's lowest terrain, separates the east and west banks of the Jordan River. The land then rises to a north-south mountain range containing Jordan's highest point. These mountains give way to a high desert plateau in the east. Its geographic position has been volatile and dangerous since independence in 1946.

People

Population: 5,759,732 **Growth rate:** 2.6%
Birth rate: 21.8 births/1,000 population
Death rate: 2.6 deaths/1,000 population
Life expectancy: 78 years
Ethnic groups: Arab 98%, Circassian 1%,
Armenian 1%
Religions: Sunni Muslim 92%, Christian 6%,
other 2%
Languages: Arabic (official), English

Jordan's culture and its language is Arabic, though English is widely used in commerce and government. Nearly three quarters of the population live in cities, and less than 6% of the rural population is nomadic or semi-nomadic. About 1.7 million people classified as Palestinian refugees and displaced persons live in Jordan, and most are Jordanian citizens.

Government

Government type:
constitutional monarchy
Capital: Amman
Admin. divisions: 12 governorates
Independence: May 25, 1946

Jordan's constitution provides for a bicameral legislature and three types of courts: civil, religious and special. The king's veto may be overridden by a two-thirds vote of both houses. King Hussein ended a long period of martial law in 1991, and legalized political parties in 1992, paving the way to free and fair parliamentary elections. Since then, the Jordanian parliament has played an increasingly important role in government. After Hussein's death in 1999, his son King Abdullah II pledged to continue his father's policies, and has focused his efforts on economic reform. For many years Jordan has pursued pro-Western policies, but relations were strained by popular support of Iraq during the Gulf War, which forced Jordan to declare a neutral position between the west and Saddam Hussein's regime.

Economy

GDP- real growth rate: 5.1%
GDP- per capita: $4,500
Currency: Jordanian dinar (JOD)

Jordan's primary exports are phosphate and potash. It lacks other natural resources, and is heavily dependent on foreign aid. During the 1990's it had to import its oil from Iraq. Lately, a pipeline from Egypt has supplied the country's crude oil needs. Favorable trade agreements enable textiles and garments made in Jordan to enter the U.S. duty and quota free. Other trade agreements with the European Union (E.U.) promise to diversify and strengthen Jordan's economy, and lessen its dependence on direct foreign aid.

Kuwait

During the 18th century, most people in Kuwait earned their living selling pearls. The development of pearl farming in Japan during the 1930's led to an economic downturn, until the discovery of oil two decades later transformed Kuwait into one of the richest countries in the world. This wealth enabled Kuwait to shake off British influence and declare itself an independent country in 1961. Iraq challenged this declaration, and threatened to invade Kuwait, but was deterred at the time by Egypt. Under Saddam Hussein, Iraq invaded Kuwait in August 1990, but was forced out by U.S.-led U.N. coalition forces in February 1991. Kuwait has spent over $5 billion dollars, much of it foreign aid, to rebuild its infrastructure and restore its economy. With this aid, Kuwait has maintained its position as an independent country in a strategically important part of the world.

Geography

Total area: 6,880 sq. mi.
(17,820 sq. km.)
Highest point: unnamed
1,004 ft. (306 m.)

A small country on the Persian Gulf, Kuwait includes the mainland and nine small islands offshore. The country has a dry, desert climate with intensely hot summers and short, cool winters. Its arid terrain is flat to slightly rolling, and is resistant to agriculture. Kuwait has no lakes or reservoirs, and uses technologically advanced desalination plants to supply fresh water from the Persian Gulf. With the exception of fish, Kuwait must import its food. This means that nearly all Kuwaiti people live in urbanized areas. The Kuwaiti capital is an important center of trade and finance. Though there are no railroads, Kuwait's freeway system is well-developed, and connects its three modern seaports with its large, international airport.

People

Population: 2,335,638 **Growth rate:** 3.4%
Birth rate: 21.9 births/1,000 population
Death rate: 2.4 deaths/1,000 population
Life expectancy: 77 years
Ethnic groups: Kuwaiti 45%, other Arab 35%,
South Asian 9%, Iranian 4%, other 7%
Religions: Muslim 85%, Christian, Hindu,
Parsi, and other 15%
Languages: Arabic (official), and English

Ethnic Kuwaitis are a minority, although 80% of the population is of Arabic descent. Many Arabs from nearby states took up residence here because of the prosperity brought by oil production after the 1940s. Because the state is so small labor is scarce, and much of its work force comes from Asian and other Arab countries. English is becoming the language of commerce and language of choice for the country's large numbers of non-Arab workers. The majority of the immigrants who live here do not become Kuwaiti citizens.

Government

Government type: constitutional monarchy
Capital: Kuwait
Admin. divisions: 6 governorates
Independence: June 19, 1961 (from U.K.)

The power of Kuwait's emir is nearly absolute. He appoints the prime minister, who is assisted by a council of ministers. The National Assembly has 50 members who are elected every four years. Until 2005, less than 15% of Kuwaiti citizens were allowed to vote. In that year parliament approved women's suffrage to take effect in 2007. This development promises to dramatically increase the percentage of eligible voters. Kuwait has also appointed a woman cabinet minister.

Economy

GDP- real growth rate: 6.8%
GDP- per capita: $21,300
Currency: Kuwaiti dinar (KD)

A massive influx of foreign aid has enabled Kuwait to repair its infrastructure and rebuild its economy in the years since the Iraqi invasion. Despite its tiny size, Kuwait has 10% of the world's proven petroleum reserves. The oil industry is owned by the government, and provides 80% of government income and 90% of export revenues. This income, though dependent on the state of the world oil market, sometimes provides Kuwait with a budget surplus. There is practically no cultivated land. Fish (especially shrimp) is the only food product Kuwait does not need to import.

Lebanon

This region was home to the Phoenicians, a seafaring culture that flourished for 2,000 years. Lebanon was part of the Roman Empire and later, after the period of the Crusades, was part of the Ottoman Empire until the League of Nations mandate put Lebanon under French control. Beirut was once known as the Paris of the Middle East, a cosmopolitan place where various Christian and Muslim sects could coexist. After 1948, the presence of increasing numbers of Palestinian refugees in Lebanon, supported by the militant PLO, upset a delicate balance of power. The collapse of the central government in 1975 led to various Maronite Christian and Palestinian militias allied with Druze and Sunni Muslims fighting it out for control of the country. When the war turned against the Maronites, Syria sent troops into Lebanon to support them. Israel invaded Lebanon in 1982 in response to continuing PLO attacks from bases in Lebanon, and did not withdraw until 2000. Although the Ta'if Accord of 1989 marked the end of the major period of fighting, Syria did not pull out its troops until 2005. Syria justified the continued presence of its troops by citing Beirut's requests for help, and a delay in the implementation of the reforms in the Ta'if Accord. Lebanon is making progress towards rebuilding its economic and political institutions after this devastating 15-year period of civil war in which more than 100,000 people were killed.

Temple of Jupiter, Lebanon

Geography

Total area: 4,015 sq. mi.
   (10,400 sq. km.)
Highest point: Qurnat as Sawdā'
   10,131 ft. (3,088 m.)

Lebanon features a Mediterranean climate with mild to cool, wet winters, and hot dry summers. A narrow coastal plain rises to the Lebanon Mountains, which fall to the Bekaa Valley dividing the Lebanon and Anti-Lebanon Mountains. The mountains experience heavy winter snows, which give the country more water than it needs, a rare fresh water surplus in a generally dry region.

People

Population: 3,836,018 **Growth rate:** 1.3%
Birth rate: 18.9 births/1,000 population
Death rate: 6.2 deaths/1,000 population
Life expectancy: 73 years
Ethnic groups: Arab 95%, Armenian 4%, other 1%
Religions: Muslim 60%, Christian 39%
Languages: Arabic (official), French, English and Armenian

Though Lebanon's population is 60% Muslim, this number includes several factions: Shi'a, Sunni, Druze, Islai'ilite, and Alawhite Muslims. The Christians are also divided into Maronite Catholic, Melkite Catholic, Armenian Orthodox, Syrian Catholic, Armenian Catholic, Roman Catholic and Protestant groups. This diversity was and is the reason for Beirut's rich cuisine, and its vibrant arts and culture. Summer festivals at Ballbeck attract large international crowds. Most Lebanese speak Arabic and French, though English is also becoming popular.

Government

Government type: republic
Capital: Beirut
Admin. divisions: 6 governorates
Independence: November 22, 1943, from League of Nations mandate under French administration

Reflecting the various ethnic groups in Lebanon at the time of independence in 1943, the informally arranged "National Pact" stipulated that Lebanon's president must be a Maronite Christian, the Prime Minister must be a Sunni Muslim, and the Speaker of the Parliament must be a Shi'a Muslim. The pact also stipulated the ratio of parliamentary seats between Christian and Muslim regions. This power sharing arrangement was formalized in the constitution in 1990, following the Ta'if agreement. Since the end of the civil war, the government of Lebanon has made strides in giving Muslims greater say in the political process, disbanding the militias, and repairing relations with Israel.

Economy

GDP- real growth rate: 4%
GDP- per capita: $5,000
Currency: Lebanese pound (LBP)

Before the civil war, Lebanon enjoyed a status as a gateway to the Middle East and noted banking hub. Despite the devastation of the civil war, Lebanon maintains its traditional unrestricted free-market, free-trade orientation and strong service sector. Tourism is on the rise. Although there is a long way to go, Lebanon retains many of the advantages that made its economy competitive in the region, including an educated and highly skilled work force. Lebanon has started to rebuild its physical and financial infrastructure, but at the cost of heavy borrowing. Lebanon's national debt stands at nearly 180% of its GDP.

Libya

Libya was a very poor country with bleak prospects until oil was discovered there in 1959. Since the nationalization of the oil industry in 1973, the health of the Libyan economy has been linked to world oil prices. In 1969, the ruling monarchy was deposed in a coup led by Col. Muammar al-Qaddafi, a leader who espouses neither Marxism nor capitalism. Theoretically, Libya is an Islamic socialist state, governed by the people in a unique form of direct democracy. However, it is clear that the military is in control. Qaddafi has supported terrorists abroad to further his ideology of Islamic socialism. In 1988, the downing of Pan Am flight 103 over Lockerbie, Scotland was linked to Libyan terrorists. Since the late 1990's, Libya has worked to normalize relations with the west, and has paid some reparations to victims of terrorist activities.

Geography

Total area: 679,362 sq. mi.
   (1,759,540 sq. km.)
Highest point: Bikkū Bitti
   7,438 ft. (2,267 m.)

Libya's three main regions are Tripolitania in the west, Fazzan in the southwest, and Cyrenaica in the east. There is a long coastal plain in the north, where temperatures are moderated by the cooling effect of the sea. This plain, though mainly arid, has several irrigated areas, and contains a large urban area around the capital, Tripoli. Further south is a mountainous zone, which encloses several separate desert plateaus. This area is dotted with several oases.

People

Population: 5,765,563 **Growth rate:** 2.3%
Birth rate: 26.8 births/1,000 population
Death rate: 3.5 deaths/1,000 population
Life expectancy: 77 years
Ethnic groups: Berber and Arab 97%, other 3%
Religion: Sunni Muslim 97%
Languages: Arabic, Italian, English

Berbers were once the chief ethnic group in Libya, but they have been largely assimilated into Arabic culture. There are scattered Berber communities, and many people in Fazzan are of mixed Berber and African descent. There are large numbers of foreign workers in Libya, attracted by labor shortages in the oil industry. Some 5% of the people live as pastoral nomads, mostly in Cyrenaica.

Government

Government type: military dictatorship
Capital: Tripoli
Admin. divisions: 34 municipalities
Independence: December 24, 1951 (from Italy)

Libya's highest official organ is the General People's Congress, consisting of representatives from local people's committees. In fact, Libya is really a military regime. Though Muammar al-Qaddafi has no official title, he is the de facto head of state. Qaddafi has been a strong Arab Nationalist, and Libya's military was an active participant in the 1973 Arab-Israeli war. Libya attempted to merge with Egypt in 1973, and Algeria and Tunisia in the mid-1980's. These efforts, while not successful, have resulted in more regional Arab cooperation. Libya has also supported terrorism abroad. Recently Libya has moved to normalize relations with the west, handing over the suspects in the Lockerbie bombing to the U.N., and paying $2.7 billion in reparations to the families of the victims. Libya has also renounced the production and use of chemical and biological weapons, and has agreed to submit to unannounced international inspections.

Economy

GDP- real growth rate: 4.9%
GDP- per capita: $6,700
Currency: Libyan dinar (LYD)

The Libyan economy depends on oil revenues. This revenue gives Libya one of the highest per capita GDPs in Africa, but little of this wealth is distributed to Libyan society. Since the lifting of sanctions, and the announced abandoning of nuclear weapons programs, Libya has made progress in the transition to a more market-based economy. The manufacturing sector has expanded into the production of petrochemicals, iron, steel and aluminum. Libya also exports natural gas, and produces gypsum, limestone and salt. Libya's lack of water has prompted a massive development project called "The Great Manmade River," designed to carry water from underground Sahara aquifers to northern cities, and to irrigate coastal areas for agriculture. The country's chief agricultural products are wheat, barley, olives, dates, citrus, vegetables, peanuts and almonds. Large numbers of sheep and goats are raised.

Morocco

Morocco was the first country to recognize the U.S. in 1777, and a treaty of friendship with the U.S. has been in effect since 1783. In 1904, European treaties, made without consulting the sultan, divided the country into French and Spanish zones. The Treaty of Fez, signed in 1912, formalized European sovereignty in the region. It divided Morocco into a French protectorate in the north, a Spanish protectorate in the south (Western Sahara), and made Tangier an international city. The French part of Morocco gained its independence in 1956. When Spain withdrew from Western Sahara in 1975, Morocco claimed the northern part. It later extended its claim to the whole of Western Sahara after the withdrawal of Mauritanian troops in 1979. The Polisario Front fought a guerrilla war contesting Morocco's claims to the region. A cease-fire agreement was signed in 1991 which is still enforced by U.N. peacekeepers. The status of Western Sahara is still in dispute, pending a U.N. referendum.

Geography

Total area: 172,414 sq. mi.
(446,550 sq. km.)
Highest point: Jebel Toubkal
13,665 ft. (4,165 m.)

Morocco's long shoreline reaches past the Strait of Gibraltar to the Mediterranean Sea. Ceuta and Melilla remain Spanish enclaves on the Moroccan coast. The Atlas Mountains form the spine of the country, dividing the settled coastal plains and fertile mountain valleys from the Sahara Desert in the southeast. Casablanca, a center of commerce and industry, is the country's leading port. Tangier is known as the gateway to Spain. Rabat is the seat of government, while Fez, once an opulent imperial city, is Morocco's cultural and religious center. The Berber city of Marrakech is a major tourist destination.

Women in traditional clothing, Morocco

People

Population: 32,725,847 Growth rate: 1.6%
Birth rate: 22.3 births/ 1,000 population
Death rate: 5.6 deaths/ 1,000 population
Life expectancy: 71 years
Ethnic groups: Arab-Berber 99%, other 1%
Religions: Muslim 99% other 1%
Languages: Arabic (official) Berber dialects,
French, Spanish

Most Moroccans are Sunni Muslims of Arab, Berber or mixed Arab-Berber heritage. Arabs invaded Morocco in the 7th and the 11th centuries, establishing their culture in the process. The official language is classical Arabic, but the local dialect is called Moroccan Arabic. About a third of the population speaks Berber, which has three different dialects. French is universally taught and remains the language of commerce and government. Spanish is a second language in the northern part of the country, while English is rapidly becoming the language of choice among educated youth throughout Morocco.

Government

Government type: constitutional monarchy
Capital: Rabat
Admin. divisions: 37 provinces, 2 wilayats
Independence: March 2, 1956 (from France)

Morocco is a constitutional monarchy. Among other responsibilities, the king can dissolve the government and deploy the military. Recent reforms included the adoption of a directly elected bicameral legislature in 1997. Parliamentary elections were held for the second time in 2002, and municipal elections were held in 2003. Opposition parties are legal, and several have formed in recent years.

Economy

GDP- real growth rate: 4.4%
GDP- per capita: $4,200
Currency: Moroccan dirham (MAD)

Morocco's largest industry is phosphate mining. Its second-largest source of income is money transferred to relatives from Moroccans living abroad. Agricultural exports include citrus, fruits, wine and fish. Other exports are clothing, transistors, fertilizers and petroleum products. Tourism is an important source of revenue. Morocco has recently signed Free Trade Agreements with the E.U. and the U.S.. Morocco has moved to enforce the U.N. convention against the production of cannabis, typically processed into hashish, an illegal trade which is Morocco's primary source of hard currency.

Oman

Oman occupies a strategic position on the Straits of Hormuz and the Gulf of Oman, and has always been a center for international trade. During much of the 19th century Oman was a major power, having possessions in Zanzibar (now Tanzania) on the African coast, and Baluchistan on the Iranian and Pakistani coasts. These were lost to Europe in the late 1800's. Oman has been a consistent friend to western countries, and has allowed its bases to be used by U.S. forces involved in ground attacks against Afghanistan in 2001. Oman is also the only oil-producing country in the Middle East that is not a member of OPEC.

Geography

Total area: 82,031 sq. mi.
(212,460 sq. km.)
Highest point: Jabal Shams
9,777 ft. (2,980 m.)

Oman is a vast desert plain with mountain ranges along the northern and southeastern coasts. Most of the people live in these regions, while the central coastal area is less populated. Oman is hot and dry in the interior, but humid along the coast, allowing for some agricultural activity. Oman has two areas that are geographically separate from the rest of the country. The Musandam peninsula occupies a strategic position overlooking the shipping lanes in the Strait of Hormuz, but is separated from the rest of Oman by part of the United Arab Emirates (U.A.E.). Wadi-e-Madhah, a 29 square mile (75 sq. km.) area located halfway between the Musandam peninsula and the rest of Oman, is entirely surrounded by the U.A.E.. Despite these geographic anomalies, much of Oman's border with the U.A.E. is not well defined.

People

Population: 3,001,583 Growth rate: 3.3%
Birth rate: 36.7 births/1,000 population
Death rate: 3.9 deaths/1,000 population
Life expectancy: 73 years
Ethnic groups: Arab, Baluchi, South Asian, African
Religions: Ibadhi Muslim 75%, Sunni Muslim,
Shi'a Muslim, Hindu
Languages: Arabic (official), English, Baluchi,
Urdi, Indian dialects

Most Omanis are Muslims of Arabic descent, but there is a large Baluchi minority of Iranian origin. As in other Arab countries where labor is scarce, many foreign workers live here, most from India, Pakistan and Iran. The official language is Arabic, but the minorities speak their own languages. Although Oman is politically friendly to the west, the Ibhadi form of Islam is strict compared to Sunni and Shi'a Islam, and western cultural influence is quite restricted.

Government

Government type: monarchy
Capital: Muscat
Admin. divisions: 3 governorates, 5 regions
Independence: 1971 (from U.K. protectorate)

The present dynastic line of Sultans dates from the expulsion of the Ottomans in 1741. Oman became a British protectorate from 1891 to 1971. The present Sultan has ruled since 1970. He has greatly improved the situation of the country, using oil wealth to modernize roads, schools, hospitals, and utilities. In 1996 the sultan instituted an elected bicameral advisory council with some legislative powers. Universal suffrage for those over 21 was instituted in 2003. 74% of the registered voters voted to elect members to fill 83 council seats. Two of those elected members were women.

Economy

GDP- real growth rate: 1.2%
GDP- per capita: $13,100
Currency: Omani rial (OMR)

Oman's economy is based on oil, but agriculture employs the majority of the people. Fertile areas on the northern and eastern coasts allow the production of dates, grains, limes, bananas, vegetables and livestock. Oil was discovered in Oman in 1962. The government bought a 60% stake in the European-owned oil partnership in 1974. Oman then moved quickly to modernize its economy and infrastructure. Oman is moving to privatize its utilities, liberalize its markets, and facilitate foreign investment. GDP improved in 2001 despite a global economic slowdown.

Pakistan

One of the cradles of civilization, Pakistan's history overlaps that of India, Afghanistan and Iran. Pakistan nurtured the Indus Valley civilization and has been part of several different empires, becoming part of the British Empire in the early 19th century. The separation of British India into Muslim Pakistan (west and east sections), and mostly Hindu India in 1947 has never been satisfactorily resolved. India and Pakistan fought two wars over the disputed region of Kashmir, in 1947-48 and 1965. A third war in 1971 eventually resulted in the east section of Pakistan becoming the separate nation of Bangladesh. Responding to nuclear weapons testing by India, Pakistan conducted its own tests in 1998. Although the dispute over Kashmir continues, recent discussions have contributed to a lessening of tensions. Pakistan is blessed with a variety of natural and cultural resources. Still a developing nation, Pakistan's economy continues to grow.

Geography

Total area: 310,403 sq. mi.
(803,940 sq. km.)
Highest point: K2 (Godwin-Austen)
28,251 ft. (8,611 m.)

Pakistan is dominated by the broad fertile Indus Valley flood plain in the center, which empties into the Arabian Sea near the large city of Karáchi, the outlying areas of Pakistan display a range of climates and topographies. In the southwest is the arid, mountainous plateau of Balochistan. In the northwest, cooler, wetter mountainous areas border Afghanistan. The Pakistani-administered areas of Kashmir contains K2, the world's second highest mountain. In the east is the Cholistan or Thar Desert on the border with India, which gives way to the low marshy areas east of the Indus delta. The fertile and broad Indus Valley sustained some of the world's earliest civilizations, at sites like Mohenjo Daro and Kot Diji. Agriculture remains important to Pakistan today.

People

Population: 162,419,946 Growth rate: 2.03%
Birth rate: 30.4 births/1,000 population
Death rate: 8.4 deaths/1,000 population
Life expectancy: 63 years
Ethnic groups: Punjabi, Sindhi, Pashtun,
Baloch, Muhajir (India partition immigrants
and their descendants)
Religions: Muslim 97% (Sunni 77%, Shi'a 20%),
Christian, Hindu and other 3%
Languages: Punjabi 48%, Sindi 12%, Siraiki
(a Punjabi variant) 10%, Pashtu 8%, Urdu
(official) 8%, Balochi, Hindko, and others 14%

Invaded and occupied by the Huns, Persians, Arabs, Turks, Mongols and Indo-Europeans, Pakistan's ethnic and religious history is quite diverse. These influences have contributed to the richness of Pakistani culture today. Pakistan is also the birthplace of Sikhism, and the Mahayna and Tantric varieties of Buddhism. Some scholars even add Hinduism to this list. Although 97% of Pakistanis are Muslim, the British partition caused the flight of seven million Muslims from India into Pakistan, and six million Hindus and Sikhs from Pakistan into India, creating a larger Muslim majority than before. Punjabis are the largest ethnic group, followed by the Sindhis and the Pashtuns, who live mostly in the large central provinces of Sindh and Punjab. Many of the smaller minority groups are found in the northern mountainous parts of the country. Along with English, Urdu is widely used as a second language, though native Urdu speakers number only a small percent of the population.

Government

Government type: federal republic
Capital: Islâmâbâd
Admin. divisions: 4 provinces, 2 territories,
parts of Kashmir
Independence: August 14, 1947 (from U.K.)

Officially a federal republic, Pakistan has had alternating periods of democratic and authoritarian military rule. Military generals ruled Pakistan from 1958 to 1971. Civilian rule resumed from 1971 to 1977, when Zulfiko Ali Bhutto was deposed by General Zia ul-Haq. When Zia was killed in a plane crash in 1988, Benazir Bhutto, daughter of Zulikfo Ali Bhutto, was elected Prime Minister. She was the youngest female head of state, and the first woman to lead a Muslim country. The current president, Pervez Musharraf, came to power in a military coup in 1999, but has since been officially elected to office.

Economy

GDP- real growth rate: 6.1%
GDP- per capita: $2,200
Currency: Pakistani rupee (PKR)

Traditionally an agricultural economy, about 28% of Pakistan's land area is cultivated and is watered by extensive irrigation systems. Pakistan's water resources include several major rivers, fed by snowmelt from some of the highest peaks in the world, as well as large underground aquifers. Cotton, wheat and rice are among the most important crops. Pakistan's economy grew strongly after independence, but experienced a severe slowdown in the 1990's. The government has recently instituted wide ranging economic reforms. These measures have helped Pakistan's economy to weather recent troubles, including sanctions, drought, tensions with India, and an influx of refugees from Afghanistan. Pakistan has a large, prosperous and growing middle class. Given the variety of scenic areas and historic sites in Pakistan, coupled with the recent lessening of tensions with India, tourism is also increasing.

Qatar

Located on a peninsula jutting into the Persian Gulf from mainland Saudi Arabia, the area was populated by nomadic clans battling each other for control of rich oyster beds. The British used Qatar as a stopping point on the route to colonial India. The discovery of oil in 1939 changed Qatar's outlook dramatically. When the U.K. ceased governing the region in 1971, Qatar declined to become part of the U.A.E.. Made prosperous by oil and natural gas revenues, Qatar is an economic power and a politically moderate force in the region. The English pronunciation of Qatar falls somewhere between "cutter" and "gutter."

Geography

Total area: 4,416 sq. mi.
(11,437 sq. km.)
Highest point: Qurayan Abū al Bawl 338 ft. (103 m.)

Much of Qatar is a low, barren desert plain covered with sand. To the west, limestone outcrops contain Qatar's highest point, as well as the country's mainland oil deposits. Gas fields are offshore to the northwest. To the southeast is the Khor al Adaid, or "Inland Sea," an area of rolling sand dunes surrounding an inlet of the Persian Gulf. Very little land is farmed.

People

Population: 863,051 **Growth rate:** 2.6%
Birth rate: 15.5 births/1,000 population
Death rate: 4.6 deaths/1,000 population
Life expectancy: 73.7 years
Ethnic groups: Arab 40%, Pakistani 18%, Iranian 10%, other 14%
Religion: Muslim 95%
Languages: Arabic (official), English

Nearly all Qataris are Muslim. Most are descended from a number of migratory tribes which came to Qatar in the 18th century to escape the harsh conditions of neighboring areas. A large majority profess the Wahhabi doctrine, a puritanical version of Islam. Wahhabi religious practice is less strict in Qatar than in Saudi Arabia, and is not generally imposed on foreigners. Much of the population emigrated from other, mostly Asian nations to work in the oil industry.

Government

Government type: constitutional monarchy
Capital: Doha
Admin. divisions: 10 municipalities
Independence: September 3, 1971 (from U.K.)

During the 19th century, Qatar was ruled by the al Khalifa clan from the offshore island of Bahrain. When the al Khalifas sent a naval force to crush Qatari rebels in 1867, the British diplomatic response lead to the recognition of Qatar as separate from Bahrain, though it did not become a protectorate until 1916. To negotiate with Great Britain, Qatar sent a representative from the Al Thani, ensuring this clan's future role as the ruling dynasty in the region, a position it holds today. Long a traditional kingdom, Qatari voters have only recently approved a constitution that defines the emir's power and enfranchises women.

Economy

GDP- real growth rate: 8.7%
GDP- per capita: $23,200
Currency: Qatari rial (QAR)

Qatar's economy has rebounded from the siphoning of oil revenues by the former emir, who spent much of his time vacationing abroad. His son deposed him in a bloodless 1995 coup, and has enacted reforms, including the drafting of a constitution and the enfranchisement of women. Qatar has the highest GDP in the developing world. This wealth allows for generous amounts of social spending, including free health care for all citizens, and free education from kindergarten through college. Qatar wants to develop a knowledge economy, and has established the Qatar Science and Technology Park to attract and serve technology-based companies. This facility will establish ties between Qatari industry and the newly established satellite campuses of several American universities. Al Jazeera, the controversial Arabic satellite news channel is based here.

Saudi Arabia

Saudi Arabia, named after the country's ruling Saud dynasty, is also called "The Land of the Two Holy Mosques," referring to Mecca, birthplace of the Prophet Mohammed, and Medina, which are Islam's two holiest places. Around 1750, Muhammad bin Saud, a regional ruler, joined forces with an Islamic reformer Muhammad Abd al Wahhab. Since then, the Saudi state has been linked with the Wahhabi practice of Islam, a more conservative practice than Shi'a or Sunni Islam. From 1902-1932, Saudi King Abdul Aziz proceeded to unify most of the peninsula under one central government. In 1932 a unified kingdom was proclaimed. Oil was discovered in 1938, transforming the economy and giving further legitimacy to Saudi rule. With the world's largest petroleum reserves and the clout to control production, Saudi Arabia remains a force in world politics, and has a standard of living comparable to that of many industrialized countries.

Annual pilgrimage to Mecca, Saudi Arabia

Geography

Total area: 856,355 sq. mi.
(1,960,582 sq. km.)
Highest point: Jabal Sawdā' 10,279 ft. (3,133 m.)

Saudi Arabia is the largest country on the Arabian Peninsula. Most of the country's boundaries with the U.A.E., Oman and Yemen are undefined, so the exact size of the country remains indefinite. The figure shown is a government estimate. The climate is dry and hot, with great extremes in temperature. In most of the country, vegetation is limited to weeds, herbs and shrubs. Almost half the country is uninhabited desert, dotted with occasional, often densely populated oases. The southwest region is known for the greenest and freshest climate in the country, but even there little farming is possible. There are no permanent rivers and lakes in Saudi Arabia. The coastal areas, especially the coral reefs, provide habitat for a rich and diverse marine life.

People

Population: 26,417,599 **Growth rate:** 2.3%
Birth rate: 29.6 births/1,000 population
Death rate: 2.6 deaths/1,000 population
Life expectancy: 75.5 years
Ethnic groups: Arab 90%, Afro-Asian 10%
Religion: Muslim 100%
Language: Arabic

Saudi Arabia's population includes about 6.4 million resident foreigners. There are significant numbers of expatriates from several Southeast Asian countries. Until the 1960's, much of the population was nomadic or semi-nomadic, but the rapid growth of the oil industry has settled most of the population in densely packed cities. Most Saudis are Arabic, but some are of mixed heritage, descended from Turks, Iranians and others who came to the region as religious pilgrims.

Government

Government type: monarchy
Capital: Riyadh
Admin. divisions: 13 provinces
Independence: September 23, 1932 (Unification of the Kingdom)

The Basic Law, adopted in 1992, stated that Saudi Arabia is a monarchy ruled by the sons and grandsons of the first king Abd Al-Aziz Al Saud, and that the Koran is the constitution of the country, which is governed on the basis of Islamic Law (Shari'a). There are no recognized political parties or national elections. However, the king must retain a consensus of the royal family, religious leaders (ulema), and other important elements in society. The leading members of the royal family choose the king from among themselves, with subsequent approval of the ulema. It is an established tradition that the people have access to high officials, usually at public audiences, and the right to petition them directly. When the new Kuwaiti voting law takes effect in 2007, Saudi Arabia will be the only Middle Eastern country that does not allow women the right to vote.

Economy

GDP- real growth rate: 5%
GDP- per capita: $12,000
Currency: Saudi riyal (SAR)

Saudi Arabia is known to have about one quarter of the world's petroleum reserves. This figure is gradually increasing as new fields are discovered. Saudi Arabia is the world's largest exporter of petroleum, and plays a leading role in OPEC. Together with other countries, it has the clout to raise the price of oil by reducing production. In recent years, the country has experienced a reduction in oil revenues combined with a large increase in population. Per capita income has fallen since 1980. The government has been privatizing government run utilities in order to increase employment in the private sector and to relieve unemployment. Despite irrigation, less than 2% of the country's land area can be cultivated. Even with the advent of modern desalinization plants, water shortages persist. Because of the depletion of underground aquifers, governmental goals to increase agricultural self-sufficiency will be difficult to achieve.

Sudan

Once known as the Nubian Kingdom, and located along the Nile from the first to the sixth cataracts of the Nile, northern Sudan was influenced by the Egypt of the Pharoahs. At times this region was indistinguishable from Upper Egypt. An Arab merchant class established itself here in the seventh century A.D. From 1898 to 1956, Britain essentially administered Sudan as two separate states. While roads and schools were built in the predominantly Arab north, the southern tribal areas were left mostly on their own. This has created cultural and economic rifts that persist to this day, contributing to decades of civil war. The Navisha peace agreement of 2005 states that the south will be granted autonomy for six years, followed by a referendum on independence.

Geography

Total area: 967,498 sq. mi.
(2,505,810 sq. km.)
Highest point: Kinyeti 10,456 ft. (3,187 m.)

Sudan is the largest country in Africa, and the tenth largest in the world. The terrain is largely flat, eventually rising to mountains in the south, northeast and west. The northern climate is that of the dry Sahara desert, and the southern climate is humid and tropical. While the north is mostly Arabic, the south is primarily an indigenous African culture. Khartoum, the capital, holds a strategic central position in relation to the Upper and Lower Nile valleys, as well as to Sudan's access to the Red Sea at Port Said. Without help from the government in Khartoum, people in the south have suffered greatly from famine and the displacement caused by a long civil war. As a result, it is estimated that two million southerners have died, and four million have lost their homes or become refugees. Many fled to southern cities, Khartoum, or to neighboring countries such as Egypt, Ethiopia, Kenya and Uganda. Southern Sudan is now an autonomous region. Darfur is a region of three western states involved in violent civil conflict since 2003.

People

Population: 40,187,486 Growth rate: 2.6%
Birth rate: 35.2 births/1,000 population
Death rate: 9.2 deaths/1,000 population
Life expectancy: 58.6 years
Ethnic groups: non-Arabic Africans 52%,
   Arabic Africans 39%, Beja 6%, other 3%
Religions: Sunni Muslim 70%,
   indigenous beliefs 25%, Christian 5%
Languages: Arabic (official), Nubian,
   Ta Bedawie, dialects of Nilotic, Nilo-Hamitic,
   and Sudanic languages, English

Sudan has two major cultures, Arabic Black Africans, and non-Arabic Black Africans. These include dozens of ethnic and tribal divisions, as well as different language groups that make working together more difficult. In northern regions, which includes most of the cities in Sudan, most of the 22 million inhabitants are Arabic speaking Muslims, although many also use a traditional non-Arabic language like Nubian or Beja. In the north, away from the cities, there are several tribal groups, including the Kababish, a camel-raising people, the semi-nomadic Baggara living in the west, and the Beja people in the area of the Red Sea. The southern region has a population of about 6 million and a predominantly rural subsistence economy. People here practice traditional indigenous beliefs. This culture is divided into many tribal groups and many more different languages than in the north. The Dinka people, numbering more than one million, are the largest of the many Black African tribes in southern Sudan. There are also another 12 million people living in the eastern and western regions of Sudan which make up the balance of Sudan's population.

Government

Government type: authoritarian regime
Capital: Khartoum
Admin. divisions: 26 states (wilayat)
Independence: January 1, 1956
   (from Egypt and U.K.)

Since independence in 1956, military regimes favoring Islamic-oriented governments have dominated Khartoum. The current regime is a mixture of military elite and an Islamist party that came to power in a 1989 coup. General Omar el-Bashir became president, chief of state, prime minister and chief of the armed forces. Sudan's state executives are appointed by Khartoum. Sudan has had troubled relations with its neighbors. Sudan supported anti-Ugandan rebels in retaliation for Ugandan support of Sudanese rebels. During the 1990's Ethiopia, Kenya and Uganda formed an alliance called "The Front Line States," to check the influence of the National Islamic Front Government. After the 1998 U.S. Embassy bombings, and the development of new oil fields originally in rebel hands, Sudan began to moderate its positions. Peace talks between southern rebels and the government continued for two years, up to the Navisha agreement of 2005. However, intertribal wars continue in the western Darfur region.

Economy

GDP- real growth rate: 6.4%
GDP- per capita: $1,900
Currency: Sudanese dinar (SDD)

Sudan is turning around a struggling economy through sound monetary policy, infrastructure improvements, and the development of its fledgling oil industry. As a result Sudan recorded its first trade surplus in 1999. Agriculture is still Sudan's most important sector, employing 80% of the work force, but due to a lack of irrigation, farms are vulnerable to drought. The chronic instability of the country, limited water and weak agricultural prices ensures that much of the population will remain poor.

Syria

Archaeologists have proved that Syria was the center of one of the most ancient civilizations on earth. From the city of Ebla, a great Semitic empire spread from the Red Sea north to Turkey and east to Mesopotamia around 2500 B.C.. Damascus is regarded as the oldest continuously inhabited city in the world, possibly settled as early as 10,000 B.C.. Though important to early Christian history, Syria has been a predominantly Muslim nation since 636 A.D.. It was ruled by the Ottoman Empire from 1517-1918. French forces then ruled the country until 1946. This period was marked by nationalist revolts, as well as infrastructure and economic development. After independence, a series of military coups undermined civilian rule and eventually led to Arab nationalist and socialist elements coming to power. After the Suez Crisis, Syria merged with Egypt to become the United Arab Republic from 1958-1961. Syria then declared its independence. The government was soon in control of the Arab nationalist Ba'ath party. However, internal dissention weakened the government. In 1970, then Minister of Defense Hafiz al-Asad ousted civilian leadership in a bloodless military coup. Asad moved quickly to consolidate Ba'athist power, but was resisted during the late 1970's by an insurgency of fundamentalist Sunnis. After the crushing of an attempted fundamentalist uprising in 1982 there has been little resistance to his regime.

Roman Theatre, Syria

Geography

Total area: 71,498 sq. mi. (185,180 sq. km.)
   (includes 1,295 sq. km.
   of Israeli-occupied territory)
Highest point: Mount Hermon 9,232 ft. (2,814 m.)

Because of differences in elevation, there is a range of climatic conditions in Syria. Though winters are very mild on the coast, the capital, Damascus, often sees snowfall. The interior is a mostly semi-arid plateau that is bisected by the fertile Euphrates river valley. The Mediterranean coastal plain rises to a north-south mountain range. The highest point, Mount Hermon, is near the Lebanese border in the southeast.

People

Population: 18,448,752 (this figure does not
   include 40,000 people in the Golan Heights)
Growth rate: 2.3%
Birth rate: 28.3 births/1,000 population
Death rate: 4.9 deaths/1,000 population
Life expectancy: 70 years
Ethnic groups: Arab 90%, Kurds,
   Armenians and others 9%
Religions: Sunni Muslim 74%, Alawite, Druze
   and other Muslim sects 16%, Christian 10%
Languages: Arabic (official), Kurdish, Armenian,
   Aramaic, Circassian widely understood

Arabs make up ninety percent of the population, including 400,000 Palestinian refugees. Most Kurds live in the northeast corner of Syria, but there are Kurdish communities in major Syrian cities as well. There is also a small Syrian Jewish community. Many of the educated Syrians speak French or English. Aramaic was the dominant language before the advent of Islam and Arabic, and it is still spoken among some of Syria's ethnic groups today. Armenian and Turkic are also spoken by a small portion of the population.

Government

Government type: republic under military regime
Capital: Damascus
Admin. divisions: 14 provinces
Independence: April 17, 1946 (from League of
   Nations Mandate under French administration)

Syria is governed by a single political party under a strong president. President Hafez al-Assad was elected by unopposed referenda seven times. When Hafez-al-Assad died in 2000, the constitution was quickly amended so his son could be legally nominated for election. Hopes for political liberalization under his son have stalled. Other parties are allowed under the banner of the National Party Front, but are dominated by the Ba'aths. Syria's parliament may criticize and amend laws, but only the executive branch can initiate legislation. Syrian participation in the 1990 coalition against Saddam Hussein marked a real turn in foreign policy, which had previously been anti-Western. Syria initially cooperated in the U.S.- led war on terrorism, but opposed war with Iraq in 2003. Since then, relations with the U.S. have deteriorated. In 2004 the U.S. imposed sanctions on Syria because of its support of terrorism, the continued presence of its troops in Lebanon, and its pursuit of weapons of mass destruction. Recently, Syria has withdrawn its troops from Lebanon, eliminating a long-standing source of tension in the region.

Economy

GDP- real growth rate: 2.3%
GDP- per capita: $3,400
Currency: Syrian pound (SYP)

Although Syria's petroleum reserves are small when compared to other Middle Eastern countries, petroleum accounts for much of Syria's export earnings. About one third of Syria's landmass is arable. The agricultural sector is recovering from several years of drought, and is benefiting from a change in governmental policy designed to stem rural migration and enhance exports. Current export crops include cotton, fruits and vegetables. The government hopes to increase irrigated farmland by one third over the next ten years. Syria has made economic reforms in hopes of signing trade agreements with the E.U., including opening private banks, cutting interest rates, and reducing some government food subsidies.

Tunisia

Tunisia's rare supply of fertile land became known as the bread basket of the Roman Empire. In the 7th century A.D., Tunisia was conquered by Arabs, and despite periodic Berber rebellions has retained a largely Muslim identity since. Just 90 miles from Italy, it was briefly occupied by Sicilians in the 12th century. Today, Tunisia is a modern Arab state friendly to western countries. Its women enjoy legal rights that are more extensive than many other Muslim nations.

Geography

Total area: 63,170 sq. mi.
   (163,610 sq. km.)
Highest Point: Jebel ech Chambi
   5,066 ft. (1,544 m.)

Tunisia is shaped like a wedge pointed south. The eastern end of the Atlas Mountains dips to a coastal plain in the northeast. This area features a temperate climate with mild, rainy winters and hot dry summers. This allows a variety of agricultural products to be grown. The fertile northern area gives way to a hot, dry central plain that merges into the Sahara desert in the south.

People

Population: 10,074,951 Growth rate: 1%
Birth rate: 15.5 births/1,000 population
Death rate: 5.1 deaths/1,000 population
Life expectancy: 74.9 years
Ethnic groups: Arab 98%, European & others 2%
Religions: Muslim 98%, Christian,
   Jewish and others 2%
Languages: Arabic (official) and French

Tunisians are descendants of indigenous Berber and Arab tribes as well as the many different peoples who have invaded or migrated to the area over the centuries, including Phoenicians, Romans, Vandals, and Muslims. Several small nomadic indigenous minorities have been assimilated into the larger culture over the years. Arabic is the official language, and is spoken by everyone, while French is spoken by nearly half of the population and is the principal language of business.

Government

Government type: republic
Capital: Tunis
Admin. divisions: 24 governorates
Independence: March 20, 1956 (from France)

Tunisia is a republic, but it is a single-party state, dominated by a strong president. Tunisia has had only two presidents since independence. After the overthrow of Tunisia's constitutional monarchy in 1957, their first president, Habib Bourguiba, was known for repressing Muslim fundamentalists and establishing rights for women. He banned polygamy and legalized divorce. He pursued a moderate, non-aligned foreign policy. Habib ruled until 1987, when his advancing age led his Prime Minister Zine El Abidine Ben Ali to depose him.

The unicameral legislature has 20% of its seats reserved for the opposition, but does not originate legislation, and usually passes bills presented by the executive with only minor changes.

Economy

GDP- real growth rate: 5.1%
GDP- per capita: $7,100
Currency: Tunisian dinar (TND)

Tunisia's economy is diverse, with important agricultural, mining, energy and manufacturing sectors. Tunisian exports include textiles, mechanical goods, phosphates and petrochemicals, as well as olives, grain, dairy and other agricultural products. Government control of the economy is still strong, but Tunisia has been moving towards economic liberalization by increasing privatization and simplifying the tax code. It plans to remove all duties and trade barriers with Europe by 2008. Tunisia's prudent approach to debt, and increasing revenue from tourism, has helped its recent economic growth.

Turkey

Modern Turkey was founded in 1923 from the remnants of the Ottoman Empire by Mustafa Kemal, later given the title Ataturk, or "Father of the Turks." After the victorious Allies sought to divide Turkey following World War I, armed resistance headed by Ataturk brought about the revocation of the Treaty of Sèvres. This resulted in the end of the Ottoman Empire, the defeat of Allied forces, and the eventual recognition of the new Turkish republic through the Treaty of Lausanne in 1923. Under Kemal's authoritarian leadership, Turkey adopted wide-ranging social, legal and political reforms. After a period of one-party rule, the 1950 election brought the opposition Democratic Party peacefully to power. Turkey's peace has been shattered since 1984 by a bloody Kurdish insurgency that has claimed 30,000 lives, and has not been resolved. In 2004, insurgents announced the end of a five-year cease fire. To prevent a Greek takeover, Turkey invaded Cyprus in 1974 capturing the northern third of the island. Since then, Turkey has supported the Turkish Republic of Northern Cyprus.

Celsus Library, Turkey

Geography

Total area: 301,383 sq. mi.
(780,580 sq. km.)
Highest point: Mount Ararat
16,949 ft. (5,166 m.)

The Asian part of Turkey, called the Anatolian peninsula, borders the Black Sea, the Aegean Sea and the Mediterranean. The Black Sea and the Aegean Sea are connected by the straits of Bosporus and the Dardanelles. The section of Turkey west of the Bosporus is geographically part of Europe. The Turkish mainland to the east is more rugged, and contains Turkey's highest peak as well as the headwaters of the Tigris and Euphrates rivers. Turkey is crisscrossed by fault lines, and is prone to major earthquakes. Turkey's climate is generally Mediterranean, with hot, dry summers, and mild wet winters, although conditions are harsher in the drier parts of the interior and the higher elevations of the mountains.

People

Population: 69,660,559
Birth rate: 16.8 births/1,000 population
Death rate: 6.0 deaths/ 1,000 population
Life expectancy: 72.4 years
Ethnic groups: Turkish 80%, Kurdish 20%
Religions: Muslim 99.8%, others 0.2%
Languages: Turkish (official), Kurdish,
Arabic, Armenian, Greek

Although more than 70% of the population is considered Turkish, this includes people from many different ethnic backgrounds. Counted among them are Albanians, Arabs, Bosnians, Chaldeans, Chechens, and Circassians, among others. Turkey considers only those communities mentioned by the Treaty of Lausanne as minorities. The largest of these groups are the Kurds, concentrated in southeastern Turkey. Though 98% of the population is Muslim (mostly Sunni), the constitution prohibits religious discrimination as well as overtly religious political parties.

Government

Government type: parliamentary democracy
Capital: Ankara
Admin. divisions: 81 provinces (il)
Independence: October 29, 1923

The president is elected for a seven-year term by the Grand National Assembly, the legislative branch of the Turkish government. Although the president is head of state, executive power rests with the Prime Minister and the Council of Ministers, who must maintain the trust and confidence of parliament. The independence of the judiciary is protected by the constitution. The Turkish Armed Forces number 635,000 troops, which is the second-largest force in the North Atlantic Treaty Organization (NATO), behind the U.S.. Turkey has been a strategic partner of the U.S. since joining NATO in 1952.

Economy

GDP- real growth rate: 8.2%
GDP- per capita: $7,400
Currency: Turkish lira (TRL)

Turkey has a dynamic economy with a complex mix of modern industry and commerce, along with a traditional agricultural sector that still accounts for more than a third of all employment. Turkey is self-sufficient agriculturally, and major crops include cotton, tobacco, citrus and the production of livestock. Turkey's most important export industry is textiles and clothing. Turkey also has a dynamic automotive industry. The state still plays a major role in basic industry, banking, transport and communication. Partly because of its large public sector, Turkey is troubled by budget deficits, debt and inflation. Turkey is applying for membership in the E.U. in hopes of increasing foreign investment.

United Arab Emirates

The U.A.E. is comprised of seven sheikdoms or emirates that granted the U.K. control of their defense and foreign affairs in the 19th century. The emirates are Abu Dhabi, Ajman, Dubai, Fujara, Ras al-Khaimah, Sharjah, and Umm-al Quwain, each ruled by a sheik. These states were formerly known collectively as the Trucial States, or Trucial Oman, referring to the treaties signed with the U.K.. After the departure of the British in 1971, these seven states merged to form the U.A.E.. Qatar was to be part of this federation, but later chose not to join. Oil revenue has transformed this formerly impoverished area into a very wealthy nation playing an important role in a strategic region of the world.

Geography

Total area: 32,000 sq. mi.
(82,880 sq. km.)
Highest point: Jabal Yibir
5,010 ft. (1,527 m.)

The U.A.E. occupies a strategic position over the shipping lanes in the Strait of Hormuz. A flat coastal plain merges into the vast, empty sand dunes of the Arabian Desert. In the east, the land rises to a mountainous region called Al Jabal al Akhdar, a range located mostly in Oman. The climate is hot and dry, though cooler conditions can be found as the land rises in the east. The U.A.E. contains some interesting geographic anomalies. There is an Omani enclave inside the U.A.E. called Wadi-e-Madhah, located halfway between the Musandam Peninsula and the large contiguous part of Oman. Within this enclave is an exclave of the U.A.E. called Nahwa, consisting of about 40 houses.

People

Population: 2,563,212
Birth rate: 18.8 births/1,000 population
Death rate: 4.3 deaths/1,000 population
Life expectancy: 75.2 years
Ethnic groups: Emirati 19%, other Arab and
Iranian 23%, South Asian 50%,
other expatriates 8%
Religions: Muslim 96%, Christian,
Hindu and other 4%
Languages: Arabic (official), Persian,
English, Hindi, Urdu

Over three-quarters of the U.A.E.'s population is not Emirati. Non-native immigrants are often referred to as expatriates. Half of this population is from south Asian countries. Arabic is the official language, but English is becoming more important. The U.A.E. has been criticized for not protecting the rights of Asian emigrant workers, not enforcing labor laws, and not having a fair immigration and naturalization policy. The U.A.E. retains strong ties with the Arab world, and is committed to preserving traditional culture. Because of an influx of tourists, social values are becoming more open and cosmopolitan, and new sports are becoming popular. The Dubai World Cup boasts horse racing's richest purse.

Government

Government type: federation of emirates
Capital: Abu Dhabi
Admin. divisions: 7 emirates (sheikdoms)
Independence: December 2, 1971 (from U.K.)

The Supreme Council, consisting of the rulers of the seven emirates, elects the president and vice president every five years. Unofficially, the presidency is hereditary to the Al-Nahyan clan of Abu Dhabi, and the premiership is hereditary to the Al-Maktoom clan of Dubai. The Supreme Council also elects the Council of Ministers, while the Federal National Council, whose 40 members are appointed from all the emirates, reviews proposed laws. All the emirates have secular and Islamic law for civil, criminal and high courts. Since independence, the U.A.E. has pursued a foreign policy friendly to the west.

Economy

GDP- real growth rate: 5.7%
GDP- per capita: $25,200
Currency: Emirati dirham (AED)

The U.A.E.'s wealth is based on oil and gas. It is the third largest oil producer in the Persian Gulf, after Saudi Arabia and Iran, and has a standard of living equal to many western European nations. Although the U.A.E.'s oil reserves should last for more than 100 years, the government has also encouraged other revenue sources, and is moving to privatize its utilities in order to create more jobs. The U.A.E. is also moving towards signing a Free Trade Agreement with the U.S.. The government has also developed spectacular tourist resorts along the coast.

Yemen

Historically a center of the spice trade, Yemen was known to the Romans as Arabia Felix (Happy Arabia). Roman attempts to annex the area failed, and Yemen became a Persian province around the year 575. In the 7th century, Islamic caliphs gained power in the region. Yemen formerly consisted of two separate countries, the Yemen Arab Republic (North Yemen) and the People's Democratic Republic of Yemen (South Yemen). At the time of unification in 1990, both were struggling, underdeveloped countries. The north was weakened by 8 years of civil war. The south was weakened by the closure of the Suez Canal from 1967 to 1975; a major economic blow at a critical time. Both countries were weakened by two decades of sporadic clashes along their common border. Since unification in 1990, work to integrate the divergent governments of north and south has been slow.

Geography

Total area: 203,850 sq. mi.
(527,970 sq. km.)
Highest point: Jabal an Nabi Shu'ayb
12,336 ft. (3,760 m.)

Yemen is a country of uplands and mountains, with a narrow coastal plain sloping up to a central plateau and the interior of the Arabian Desert. The climate is hot and humid along the western coast and temperate in western mountainous areas affected by seasonal Monsoon winds. Elsewhere the climate is mostly hot and dry. Most of the people live in the interior plateau, where cotton, coffee and other crops are cultivated. However, the Yemeni economy is still dependent on the price of oil. Yemen also includes the island of Socotra, in the Gulf of Aden off the Somali coast.

People

Population: 20,727,063 **Growth rate:** 3.4%
Birth rate: 43.1 births/1,000 population
Death rate: 8.5 deaths/1,000 population
Life expectancy: 61.8 years
Ethnic groups: predominantly Arab, but also
    Afro-Arab, South Asians and Europeans
Religions: Muslim, both Sunni and Shi'a, and
    small numbers of Jewish, Christian and Hindu
Language: Arabic

Unlike other people on the Arabian Peninsula, Yemenis have always been sedentary, living in small villages or towns. After unification, 850,000 Yemenis returned to their homeland from neighboring states. Yemen also has a very high birth rate, twice the rate of more modernized Arab countries. Arabic is the official language, though English is increasingly used in urban areas. In the Mahra area in the east several non-Arabic languages related to Ethiopian are spoken, while on the island of Socotra, one Ethiopian-based language, Soqotri, is found.

Government

Government type: republic
Capital: Sanaa
Admin. divisions: 19 governorates (muhafazat)
Independence: May 22, 1990
    Republic of Yemen established
    The Yemen Arab Republic (North Yemen) merged with the People's Democratic Republic (South Yemen).

The north part of Yemen became independent from the Ottoman Empire in 1918, but was ruled by a king until 1962, when an eight-year war was fought between royalists and republicans. Saudi Arabia supported the royalists during this war, but gave North Yemen substantial budgetary support after recognizing the Yemen Arab Republic in 1970.

In the south, after violence from the pro-independence National Liberation Front, the U.K. left Aden in 1967, and the People's Democratic Republic of Yemen was proclaimed. The new Marxist based government had strained relations with its Arab neighbors. The exodus of thousands of Yemenis from the south to the north during this period contributed to two decades of hostilities and border clashes between the states. The government of the unified Republic of Yemen is a republic with an elected bicameral legislature. An elected president, an elected 301-seat parliament, and an appointed 111-member Shura council share power. Yemen has pursued a non-aligned foreign policy, abstaining from U.N. Security Council votes concerning Iraq and Kuwait, and voting against the use of force. Subsequently, it maintained relations with Iraq. This strained relations with its Arab neighbors, but since 1994, Yemen has been working to repair its relationships in the region.

Minaret mosque, Yemen

Economy

GDP- real growth rate: N/A (government has
    reported strong growth since 2000)
GDP- per capita: $800
Currency: Yemeni rial (YER)

Coffee used to be the north's main export. But the disruptions of an 8-year civil war, and frequent periods of drought, have dealt severe blows to a formerly prosperous sector, and led to increased production of qat, a mildly narcotic shrub. Yemen has worked to modernize and streamline its economy, to control government spending and restructure its foreign debt. Yemen hopes to increase tourism and encourage more efficient use of scarce water resources, but continuing internal dissention makes progress difficult. Most of Yemen's income is from oil, but due to a vulnerable agriculture sector, Yemen remains one of the poorest countries in the Arab world.

West Bank and Gaza Strip

Both the West Bank and Gaza Strip are not legally recognized as part of any country, and are considered by the U.N. to be occupied by Israel. Both territories are thought of as important parts of a future Palestinian state by the four powers proposing The Road Map for Peace, namely the U.N., the U.S., Russia, and the E.U..

West Bank

Geography

Total area: 3,629 sq. mi.
    (5,840 sq. km.)
Highest point: Tall 'Āsūr
    3,353 ft. (1,022 m.)

In English, the West Bank is also called Judea and Samaria. The territory is known as Cisjordan "this side of the Jordan," by French and Spanish speakers. Topographically, the area is dominated by a mountainous central spine, where the cities of East Jerusalem, Nablus, and Ramallah are located. The climate is temperate, but subject to variations due to differences in elevation. The vegetation becomes more sparse and barren towards the eastern part of the territory. More than a third of the West Bank is under the limited civilian jurisdiction of the Palestinian Authority. Israel retains overall control of the region but, except for East Jerusalem, it has not annexed it. After the breakup of the Ottoman Empire, the area became part of the British mandate of Palestine. From 1948 it was controlled by Jordan until its capture by Israel during the Arab-Israeli War of 1967. As part of the 2004 peace accord with Israel, Jordan has relinquished its territorial claim to the West Bank.

People

Population: 2,800,000 **Growth rate:** 3.1%
Birth rate: 32.3 births/1,000 population
Death rate: 4.0 deaths/1,000 population
Life expectancy: 73 years
Ethnic groups: Palestinian Arab 83%, Israeli 17%
Religions: Muslim (predominantly Sunni),
    Jewish 17%, Christian and other 8%
Languages: Arabic, Hebrew, English

The West Bank territory is ethnically divided. Palestinians live in Palestinian villages, while most Israelis live in Jewish settlements, though some Jewish populations do exist in the Arab neighborhoods of Jerusalem and Hebron. About a third of the Palestinians living in the West Bank are refugees or their descendents who fled or were expelled from Israel during the 1948 Arab-Israeli War.

Government

Government type: occupied territory

Much of the West Bank, including most Palestinian villages, is under the civilian control of the Palestinian Authority. Israel maintains control of the Jewish settlements, as well as the rural and border regions, and retains overall military control of the region. Both Palestinian and Jewish people consider Jerusalem their capital.

Economy

GDP- real growth rate: 6%
GDP- per capita: $754
Currency: New Israeli Shekel

Irrigation projects have helped make some of the West Bank arable. Agricultural products include olives, citrus, and vegetables, as well as beef and dairy products. The economy of the West Bank is subject to Israeli limitations on Palestinian employment, travel and housing, imposed because of security concerns. Because of the recent destruction of infrastructure due to Israeli military measures, the West Bank is very dependent on foreign aid. In 2004, more than half of the population lived below the poverty line. Though interactions between Palestinian and Jewish societies have declined, an economic relationship often exists between adjacent Israeli settlements and Palestinian villages. Some small scale industries have been established in the settlements and cities of the West Bank.

Gaza Strip

Geography

Total area: 224 sq. mi. (360 sq. km.)
Highest point: Abu 'Awdah 344 ft. (105 m.)

The Gaza Strip is an area bordering the Mediterranean Sea with mild winters and hot, dry summers. The climate is temperate but the land is subject to drought. Terrain is flat or rolling, with dunes near the coast.

People

Population growth rate: 2.8%
Birth rate: 30.8 births/1,000 population
Death rate: 3.2 deaths/1,000 population
Life expectancy: 72 years
Ethnic groups: Palestinian Muslim 99%,
    Palestinian Christian 1%
Religions: Palestinian Muslim 99%,
    Palestinian Christians 1%
Languages: Arabic, Hebrew, English

The territory is one of the most densely populated areas in the world. Upon the evacuation of the Israeli settlements in 2005, the population is now almost entirely Palestinian Muslim, with a very small minority of Palestinian Christians. The majority are Israeli refugees from the 1948 Arab-Israeli War or their descendants. Hebrew was spoken by the Israeli settlers, and many Palestinians still speak the language. English is also widely understood.

Government

Government type: occupied territory

The Gaza Strip is under the civilian control of the Palestinian Authority. Israel retains control of the airspace in the region, as well as all maritime traffic. The Palestinian people who live in the area consider Jerusalem their capital.

Economy

GDP- real growth rate: -35%
GDP- per capita: $625
Currency: New Israeli Shekel

Almost a third of the land in the Gaza Strip is arable. The main agricultural products are olives, citrus, vegetables, and beef and dairy products. Industries in the territory are often small family businesses that produce textiles, soap, olivewood carvings and mother-of-pearl souvenirs. The economy of the Gaza Strip is subject to disruption due to Israeli border closures. Widespread poverty, unemployment, and a lack of infrastructure, exacerbated by a very high birth rate, all lead to poor living conditions.

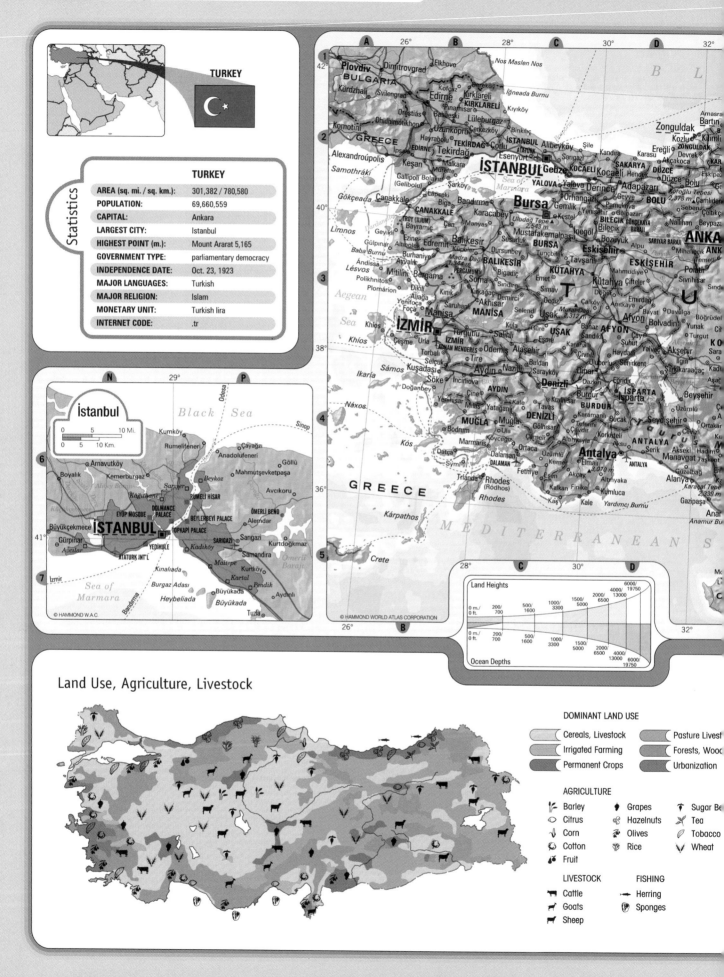

TURKEY

Statistics

TURKEY	
AREA (sq. mi. / sq. km.):	301,382 / 780,580
POPULATION:	69,660,559
CAPITAL:	Ankara
LARGEST CITY:	Istanbul
HIGHEST POINT (m.):	Mount Ararat 5,165
GOVERNMENT TYPE:	parliamentary democracy
INDEPENDENCE DATE:	Oct. 23, 1923
MAJOR LANGUAGES:	Turkish
MAJOR RELIGION:	Islam
MONETARY UNIT:	Turkish lira
INTERNET CODE:	.tr

İstanbul

© HAMMOND W.A.C.

© HAMMOND WORLD ATLAS CORPORATION

Land Heights

Ocean Depths

Land Use, Agriculture, Livestock

DOMINANT LAND USE

- Cereals, Livestock
- Irrigated Farming
- Permanent Crops
- Pasture Livest
- Forests, Wood
- Urbanization

AGRICULTURE

- Barley
- Citrus
- Corn
- Cotton
- Fruit
- Grapes
- Hazelnuts
- Olives
- Rice
- Sugar Be
- Tea
- Tobacco
- Wheat

LIVESTOCK

- Cattle
- Goats
- Sheep

FISHING

- Herring
- Sponges

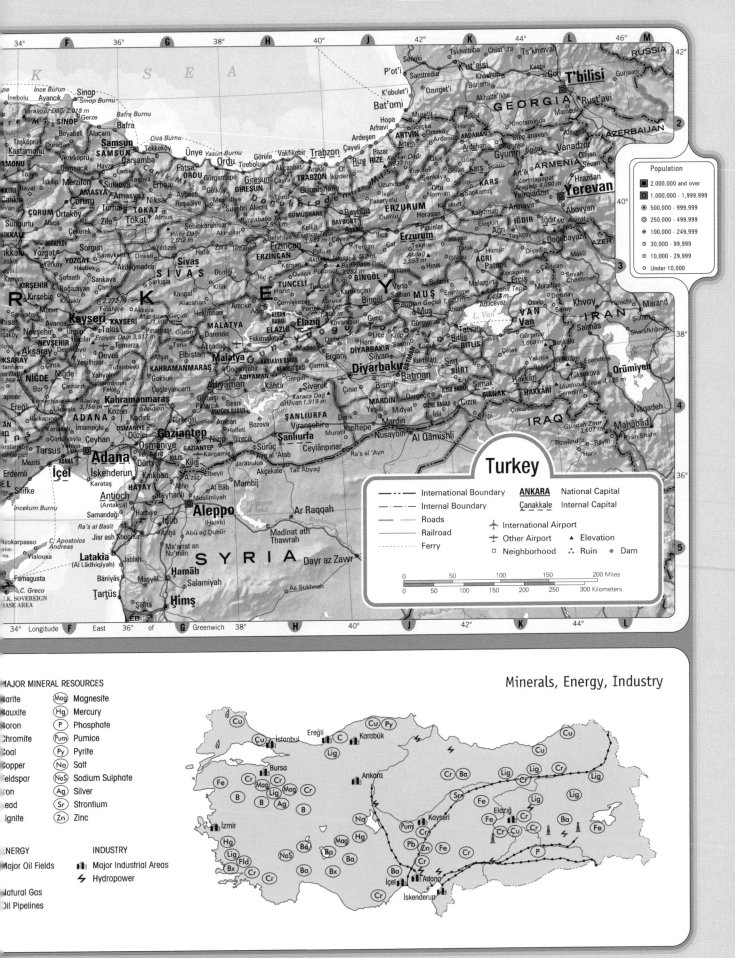

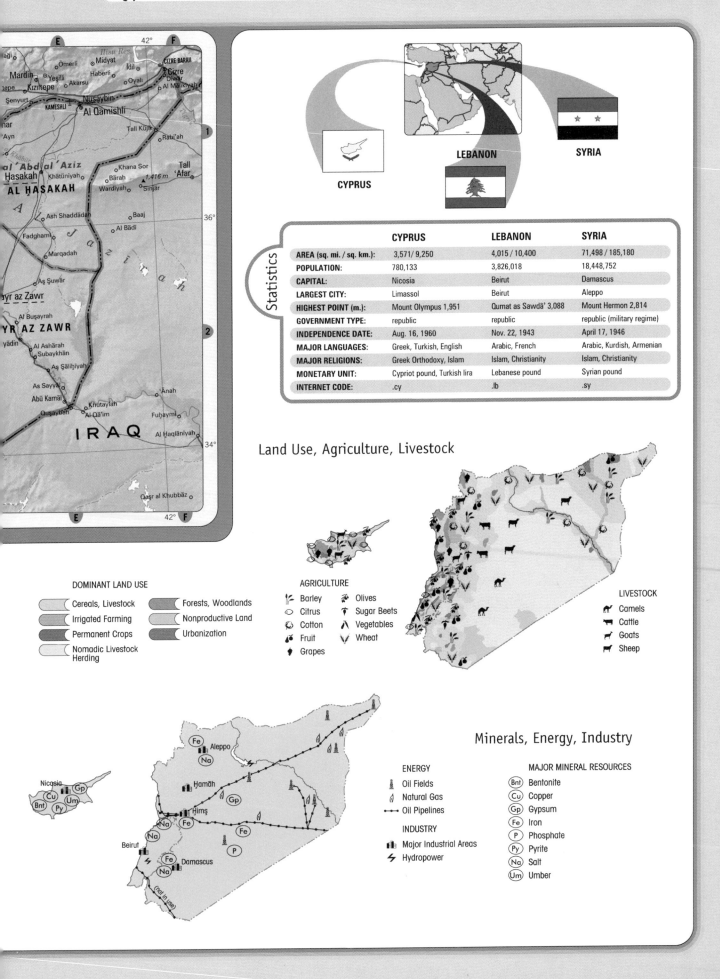

Statistics

	CYPRUS	LEBANON	SYRIA
AREA (sq. mi. / sq. km.):	3,571 / 9,250	4,015 / 10,400	71,498 / 185,180
POPULATION:	780,133	3,826,018	18,448,752
CAPITAL:	Nicosia	Beirut	Damascus
LARGEST CITY:	Limassol	Beirut	Aleppo
HIGHEST POINT (m.):	Mount Olympus 1,951	Qurnat as Sawdā' 3,088	Mount Hermon 2,814
GOVERNMENT TYPE:	republic	republic	republic (military regime)
INDEPENDENCE DATE:	Aug. 16, 1960	Nov. 22, 1943	April 17, 1946
MAJOR LANGUAGES:	Greek, Turkish, English	Arabic, French	Arabic, Kurdish, Armenian
MAJOR RELIGIONS:	Greek Orthodoxy, Islam	Islam, Christianity	Islam, Christianity
MONETARY UNIT:	Cypriot pound, Turkish lira	Lebanese pound	Syrian pound
INTERNET CODE:	.cy	.lb	.sy

CYPRUS   LEBANON   SYRIA

Land Use, Agriculture, Livestock

DOMINANT LAND USE

- Cereals, Livestock
- Irrigated Farming
- Permanent Crops
- Nomadic Livestock Herding
- Forests, Woodlands
- Nonproductive Land
- Urbanization

AGRICULTURE

- Barley
- Citrus
- Cotton
- Fruit
- Grapes
- Olives
- Sugar Beets
- Vegetables
- Wheat

LIVESTOCK

- Camels
- Cattle
- Goats
- Sheep

Minerals, Energy, Industry

ENERGY

- Oil Fields
- Natural Gas
- Oil Pipelines

INDUSTRY

- Major Industrial Areas
- Hydropower

MAJOR MINERAL RESOURCES

- (Bnt) Bentonite
- (Cu) Copper
- (Gp) Gypsum
- (Fe) Iron
- (P) Phosphate
- (Py) Pyrite
- (Na) Salt
- (Um) Umber

Israel, West Bank and Gaza Strip

| International Boundary |
| Internal Boundary |
| Roads |
| Railroad |
| Canal |

Jerusalem National Capital
Beersheba Internal Capital

✈ International Airport
✛ Other Airport
▲ Elevation
∴ Ruin

0   10   20   30 Miles
0 10 20 30 40 Kilometers

Population
■ 2,000,000 and over
▫ 1,000,000 - 1,999,999
◉ 500,000 - 999,999
◎ 250,000 - 499,999
⊕ 100,000 - 249,999
⊕ 30,000 - 99,999
◉ 10,000 - 29,999
○ Under 10,000

MEDITERRANEAN

SEA

LEBANON

SYRIA

GOLAN HEIGHTS (OCCUPIED BY ISRAEL)

Lake Tiberias

WEST BANK

CENTRAL

Tel Aviv-Yafo

Jerusalem (Yerushalayim)

NORTHERN

Haifa (Hefa)

Nazareth (Nazerat)

Amman

JORDAN

Dead Sea -407 m

ISRAEL

GAZA STRIP
Gaza (Ghazzah)
Khān Yūnus
Rafah

Beersheba (Be'er Sheva')

Dimona

SOUTHERN

EGYPT

Sinai

Negev

© HAMMOND WORLD ATLAS CORPORATION

MAP CONTINUED IN INSET AT RIGHT

Longitude East 35° of Greenwich

Land Heights
| 6000/ 19750 |
| 4000/ 13000 |
| 2000/ 6500 |
| 1500/ 5000 |
| 1000/ 3300 |
| 500/ 1600 |
| 200/ 700 |
| 0 m./ 0 ft. |

Ocean Depths

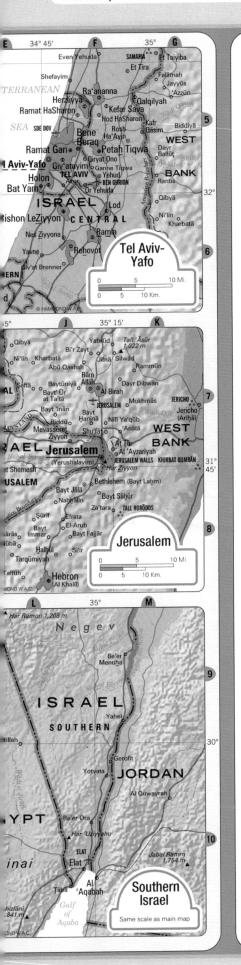

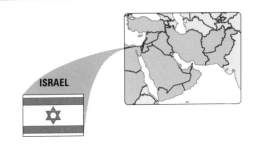

ISRAEL

Statistics

	ISRAEL	WEST BANK	GAZA STRIP
AREA (sq. mi. / sq. km.):	8,019 / 20,770	2,263 / 5,860	139 / 360
POPULATION:	6,276,883	2,385,615	1,376,289
CAPITAL:	Jerusalem	*	*
LARGEST CITY:	Tel Aviv-Yafo	Jerusalem	Gaza
HIGHEST POINT (m.):	Har Meron 1,208	Tall 'Āsūr 1,022	Abū 'Awdah 105
GOVERNMENT TYPE:	parliamentary democracy	*	*
INDEPENDENCE DATE:	May 14, 1948	*	*
MAJOR LANGUAGES:	Hebrew, Arabic	Arabic, Hebrew	Arabic, Hebrew
MAJOR RELIGIONS:	Judaism, Islam, Christianity	Islam, Christianity	Islam
MONETARY UNIT:	new Israeli shekel	new Isr. shekel, Jor. dinar	new Israeli shekel
INTERNET CODE:	.il	.ps	.ps

* West Bank and Gaza Strip are Israeli-occupied with current status subject to the Israeli-Palestinian Interim Agreement. Permanent status to be determined.

Land Use, Agriculture, Livestock

DOMINANT LAND USE

- Cereals, Livestock
- Irrigated Farming
- Permanent Crops
- Nomadic Livestock Herding
- Forests, Woodlands
- Nonproductive Land
- Urbanization

AGRICULTURE

- 🌾 Barley
- 🍊 Citrus
- 🌿 Cotton
- 🍓 Fruit
- 🍇 Grapes
- 🌿 Olives
- 🌱 Vegetables
- 🌾 Wheat

LIVESTOCK

- 🐄 Cattle
- 🐐 Goats
- 🐑 Sheep

Minerals, Energy, Industry

MAJOR MINERAL RESOURCES

- (Br) Bromine
- (Cu) Copper
- (Gp) Gypsum
- (P) Phosphate
- (K) Potash
- (Na) Salt

ENERGY

- Oil Fields
- Natural Gas
- ••• Oil Pipelines

INDUSTRY

- 🏭 Major Industrial Areas

MEDITERRANEAN SEA

LEBANON

S Y R I A

Population

■ 2,000,000 and over
☐ 1,000,000 - 1,999,999
⊙ 500,000 - 999,999
⊘ 250,000 - 499,999
⊕ 100,000 - 249,999
⊕ 30,000 - 99,999
⊕ 10,000 - 29,999
○ Under 10,000

Sidon
Damascus
Jaramānah
Buḥayrat al 'Utaybah
Qaṭanā
Dārayyā
Harrān al 'Awāmid
Mt. Hermon 2,814 m
Al Kiswah
Aş Şarafand
Marj 'Uyūn
Tyre
UNFOR
Sa'sa'
Burāq
Ar Rashidīyah
Qiryat Shemona
Jabal 'Āmil 764 m
An Nāqūrah
Al Qunayṭirah
Khan Arnabah
Jabāghib
Rosh HaNiqra
Malkiyya
Hazor
GOLAN HTS.
Aş Şanamayn
Al Jibāb
Khabab
Nahariyya
Har Meron 1,208 m
Ar Rafid
Inkhil
Acre
Karmi'el
Maghār
Zefat (OCC. BY ISR.)
Izra'
Shahbā
Jabal al 'Arab
Haifa
Qiryat Yam
Fiq
Nawā
Rosh HaKarmel
Qiryat Bialik
Tiberias
Shaykh Miskin
Tirat Karmel
Qiryat Ata
Nazareth
Nazerat 'Illit
Ar Rafid
Da'il
As Suwaydā'
Har Karmel 546 m
Dāliyat el Karmil
Afiqim
At Turrah
Jabal ad Durūz 1,803 m
El Fureidis
Afula
At Tayyibah
Irbid
Dar'ā
Ar Ramthā
Khirbat Jabir
Ar Ruwayshid
Zubūba
Bet She'an
IRBID
Hawwārah
Samā
Tisīyah
Mahaṭṭa al Jufūr
Umm el Fahm
Janīn
Dayr Abū Sa'īd
Al Ḥisn
Al Ghārīyah
'Ajjah
Qaffin
AJLŪN
Sūf
Aydūn
Al Mafraq
Sabḥā
Netanya
Qabāṭiyah
Tūbās
Kufrinjah
JARASH
Bal'amā
AL MAFRAQ
Herzliyya
Tūlkarm
Jabal 'Ajlūn 940 m
Jarash
Jubbah
KHIRBAT UMM AL JIMĀL
Kefar Sava
Kurayyimah
Anjarah
Nablus
Qalansuwa
KING TALAL DAM
Abū Nuṣayr
Al Hāshimīyah
Ramat Gan
Bene Beraq
Qabalān
AL BALQĀ'
Az Zarqā'
Tel Aviv-Yafo
Petah Tiqwa
WEST BANK (OCC. BY ISR.)
As Salt
Suwaylih
AZ ZARQĀ'
Bat Yam
Holon
Al Fuhays
Ar Ruṣayfah
Jabal Naṣlah
Rishon LeZiyyon
Bi'r Zayt
Wādī As Sīr
Amman ('Ammān)
Jabal al Ashqif
Lod
Ramla
Tall 'Asur 1,022 m
Na'ūr
Umm as Summāq
Sahab
Al Azraq ash Shāmāli
Rehovot
Biddū
Dayr Dibwān
Azraq ash Shishān
Ashdod
Jerusalem
Moza 'Illit
Har Ziyyon
Mādabā
Al Manja
Mā'īn
QUEEN ALIA INT'L
Al 'Umari
Qiryat Mal'akhi
Bethlehem
Bayt Sāḥūr
MĀDABĀ
Al Jīzah
Jabal Naṭil 802 m
Wādī Mudaysisah
Ashqelon
Qiryat Gat
Halhūl
MUKĀWIR
Al Judayyidah
Al Qunayṭirah
Jabal al Mudaysisāt 961 m
Jabal Naṣlah
Jabālyah
Gaza
Dūrā
Mukāwir
Dhībān
Mahaṭṭat Dab'ah
'AMMĀN
Al Ḥadīthah
GAZA STRIP (OCC. BY ISR.)
Sederot
Hebron
'En Gedi
Dead Sea
Fuqū'
Jabal al Jaw'alīyāt 964 m
Kāf
Khān Yūnus
Netivot
Yattah
Al Mazra'ah
Al Qasr
JORDAN
Rafah
Bani Suhaylah
Az Zāhirīyah
Adh Dhirā'
Al Karak
Qa' al Ḥafīrah
Nir Yizhaq
Ofaqim
Omer
Arad
'Ayy
AL KARAK
Beersheba
Nevatim
Newe Zohar
At Tayyibah
Revivim
Hare Dimona 681 m
Sedom
Mazār
Mu'tah
Dimona
As Safi
Jibāl Waqf aş Şawwān
Ard aş Şawwān
Wādī as Sirha
Nizzana
Oron
At Tafilah
Al Hasā
Bā'ir
Sede Boqer
Hare Hatira 716 m
Hazeva
Buşayra
Dānā
ISRAEL
En Yahav
AT TAFĪLAH
Tuwayyil ash Shihāq
Jibāl al Adhirīyāt
Mizpe Ramon
Ash Shawbak
Al Husayniyah
MA'ĀN
Har Ramon 1,208 m
Negev
BATRĀ
Wādī Mūsā
Al Jafr
Jibāl Hadra
Be'er Menuha
Ma'an
EGYPT
Gerofit
Ra's An Naqb
Qa' al Jafr
Sinai
Yotvata
Al Quwayrah
SAUDI ARABIA
Be'er Ora
AL 'AQABAH
Al Busayṭāh
Elat
Al 'Aqabah
Jabal Ramm 1,734 m
Haql
Al Mudawwarah
At Ṭubayq
Gulf of Aqaba
Nuwaybi'

© HAMMOND WORLD ATLAS CORPORATION

Land Heights

| 0 m. / 0 ft. | 200/ 700 | 500/ 1600 | 1000/ 3300 | 1500/ 5000 | 2000/ 6500 | 4000/ 13000 | 6000/ 19750 |

Ocean Depths

| 0 m. / 0 ft. | 200/ 700 | 500/ 1600 | 1000/ 3300 | 1500/ 5000 | 2000/ 6500 | 4000/ 13000 | 6000/ 19750 |

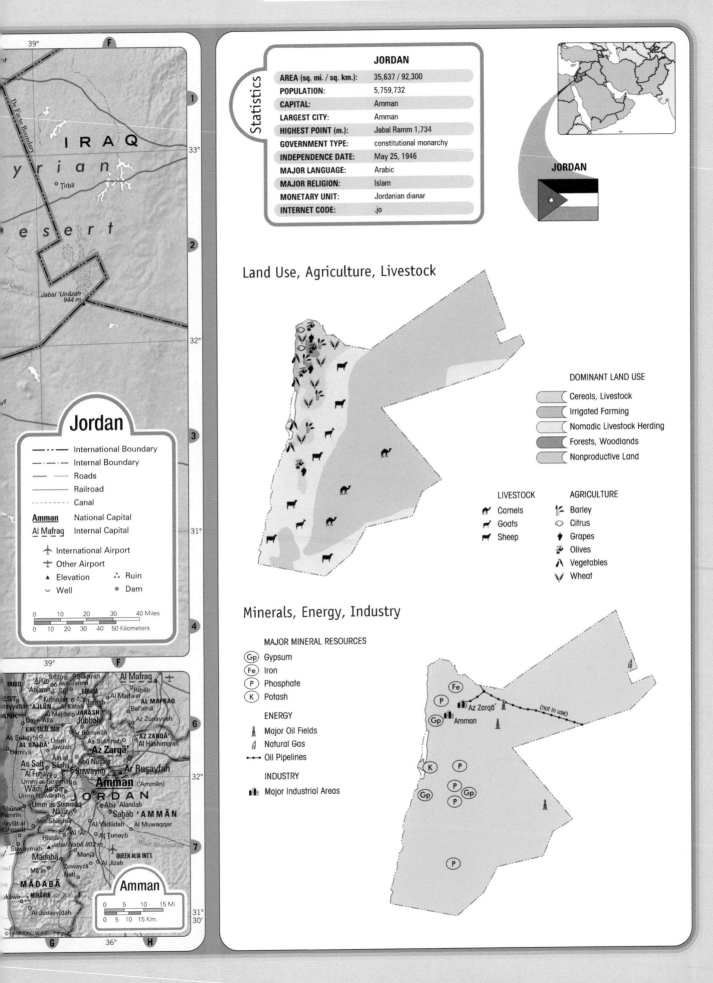

Statistics

JORDAN

AREA (sq. mi. / sq. km.):	35,637 / 92,300
POPULATION:	5,759,732
CAPITAL:	Amman
LARGEST CITY:	Amman
HIGHEST POINT (m.):	Jabal Ramm 1,734
GOVERNMENT TYPE:	constitutional monarchy
INDEPENDENCE DATE:	May 25, 1946
MAJOR LANGUAGE:	Arabic
MAJOR RELIGION:	Islam
MONETARY UNIT:	Jordanian dianar
INTERNET CODE:	.jo

JORDAN

Land Use, Agriculture, Livestock

DOMINANT LAND USE
- Cereals, Livestock
- Irrigated Farming
- Nomadic Livestock Herding
- Forests, Woodlands
- Nonproductive Land

LIVESTOCK
- Camels
- Goats
- Sheep

AGRICULTURE
- Barley
- Citrus
- Grapes
- Olives
- Vegetables
- Wheat

Minerals, Energy, Industry

MAJOR MINERAL RESOURCES
- Gp Gypsum
- Fe Iron
- P Phosphate
- K Potash

ENERGY
- Major Oil Fields
- Natural Gas
- Oil Pipelines

INDUSTRY
- Major Industrial Areas

Jordan

—··—··—	International Boundary
—·—·—	Internal Boundary
— — —	Roads
———	Railroad
·········	Canal
Amman	National Capital
Al Mafraq	Internal Capital
✈	International Airport
✚	Other Airport
▲	Elevation
⌄	Well
∴	Ruin
●	Dam

0   10   20   30   40 Miles
0   10   20   30   40   50 Kilometers

Amman

0   5   10   15 Mi.
0   5   10   15 Km.

© HAMMOND W & Co.

Statistics

	BAHRAIN	OMAN	QATAR
AREA (sq. mi. / sq. km.):	253 / 655	82,031 / 212,460	4,416 / 11,437
POPULATION:	688,345	3,001,583	863,051
CAPITAL:	Manama	Muscat	Doha
LARGEST CITY:	Manama	Muscat	Doha
HIGHEST POINT (m.):	Jabal ad Dukhān 122	Jabal Shams 2,980	Qurayn Abū al Bawl 103
GOVERNMENT TYPE:	constitutional hereditary monarchy	monarchy	traditional monarchy
INDEPENDENCE DATE:	Aug. 15, 1971	1650	Sept. 3, 1971
MAJOR LANGUAGE:	Arabic	Arabic	Arabic
MAJOR RELIGION:	Islam	Islam	Islam
MONETARY UNIT:	Bahraini dinar	Omani rial	Qatari rial
INTERNET CODE:	.bh	.om	.qa

	SAUDI ARABIA	UNITED ARAB EMIRATES	YEMEN
AREA (sq. mi. / sq. km.):	756,981/ 1,960,582	32,000 / 82,880	203,849 / 527,970
POPULATION:	26,417,599	2,563,212	20,727,063
CAPITAL:	Riyadh	Abu Dhabi	Sanaa
LARGEST CITY:	Riyadh	Dubayy	Sanaa
HIGHEST POINT (m.):	Jabal Sawdā' 3,133	Jabal Yibir 1,527	Jabal an Nabī Shu'ayb 3,760
GOVERNMENT TYPE:	monarchy	federation	republic
INDEPENDENCE DATE:	Sept. 23, 1932	Dec. 2, 1971	May 22, 1990
MAJOR LANGUAGE:	Arabic	Arabic	Arabic
MAJOR RELIGION:	Islam	Islam	Islam
MONETARY UNIT:	Saudi riyal	Emirati dirham	Yemeni rial
INTERNET CODE:	.sa	.ae	.ye

Land Use, Agriculture, Livestock

DOMINANT LAND USE

- Cereals, Livestock
- Irrigated Farming, Oases
- Pasture Livestock
- Nomadic Livestock Herding
- Forests, Woodlands
- Nonproductive Land

AGRICULTURE

- ○ Citrus
- ✗ Coffee
- ✿ Cotton
- ✽ Dates
- ☙ Fruit
- ● Grapes
- ✺ Millet
- ✽ Sorghum
- ✐ Tobacco
- ∧ Vegetables
- ∨ Wheat

LIVESTOCK

- 🐫 Camels
- 🐂 Cattle
- 🐐 Goats
- 🐑 Sheep

Minerals, Energy, Industry

MAJOR MINERAL RESOURCES

- (Cr) Chromite
- (Cu) Copper
- (Au) Gold
- (Gp) Gypsum
- (Fe) Iron
- (Pb) Lead
- (Mrb) Marble
- (P) Phosphate
- (Na) Salt
- (Ag) Silver
- (Zn) Zinc

ENERGY

- ⚒ Major Oil Fields
- ⚒ Other Oil Fields
- ◊ Natural Gas
- ⊷ Oil Pipelines

INDUSTRY

- 🏭 Major Industrial Areas

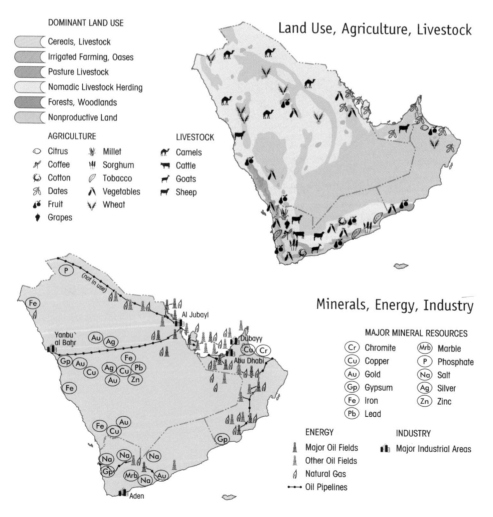

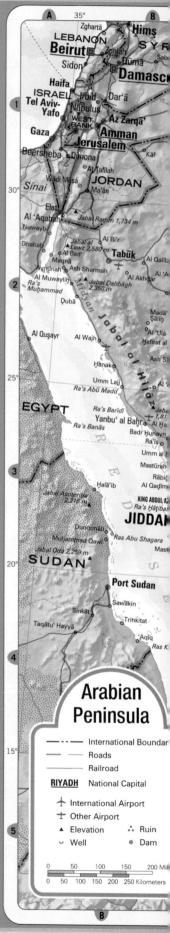

Arabian Peninsula

- ▬▬ International Boundary
- ▬ ▬ Roads
- ▬▬ Railroad
- **RIYADH** National Capital
- ✈ International Airport
- ✛ Other Airport
- ▲ Elevation
- ∴ Ruin
- ◡ Well
- ● Dam

0   50   100   150   200 Mi
0 50 100 150 200 250 Kilometers

BAHRAIN

QATAR

SAUDI ARABIA

YEMEN

UNITED ARAB EMIRATES

OMAN

Map Labels

IRAQ
bū Kamāl
Tikrīt
Al Hadīthah
Sāmarrā'
Jalūlā'
Ba'qūbah
Al Miqdādīyah
Ar Ramādī
BAGHDAD
Ar Rutbah
Tulayḥah
Unāzah
Al Hillah
Al Kūt
Ad Dīwānīyah
Karbalā'
Ash Shināfīyah
An Najaf
Ar Rifā'ī
Al 'Amārah
'Ar'ar
As Samāwah
An Nāşirīyah
Al Başrah
Khorramshahr
Al Faw
As Salmān
Al Qurnah
Ābādān

IRAN
Hamadān
Kermānshāh
Īlām
Borūjerd
Khorramābād
Andimeshk
Aḥvāz

KUWAIT
Kuwait
As Sālimīyah
Al Aḥmadī

SAUDI ARABIA
Nafūd
Jabal Shammar
Jubbah
Ḥā'il
Burayḍah
Ad Dahnā
As Summān
474 m
Ash Shumlūl
Ad Dammām
Al Khubar
Al Hufūf
Al Mubarraz
Najd
RIYADH (Ar Riyāḍ)
Al Kharj
Al Dilam
SAUDI ARABIA
ARABIAN PENINSULA
Rub' al Khali
NO DEFINED BOUNDARY
183 m
73 m

BAHRAIN
Manama (Al Manāmah)
BAHRAIN INT'L

QATAR
Ar Rayyān
Doha (Ad Dawḥah)

UNITED ARAB EMIRATES
Abu Dhabi (Abū Ȥaby)
ABU DHABI INT'L
Dubayy
DUBAI INT'L
Ash Shāriqah
SHARJAH
Ajmān
Ra's al Khaymah
RAS AL KHAYMAH
Khawr Fakkān
Al Fujayrah
Al 'Ayn
Al Buraymī

IRAN (east)
Bandar 'Abbās
Qeshm
Kūh-e Būniken 2,185 m
Kūh-e Nokhowch 2,110 m
Maskūtān
Īrānshahr
Nīkshahr
Chābahār
Bir-e 'Olyā

OMAN
Jabal Yibir 1,527 m
Al Khāburah
As Suwayq
Muscat (Masqat)
Matraḥ
SEEB INT'L
Jabal Shams 2,980 m
Ṣuḥār
Nizwā
Izki
Ibrā'
Adam
Al Kāmil
Ra's al Ḥadd
Ra's Jibsh
Dawwah
Khalūf
Jazīrat Maşīrah
Gulf of Maşīrah
Duqm
OMAN
Al Jawārah
Ra's al Madrakah
Ghubbat Şawqirah
Ra's Şawqirah
Ra's ash Sharbatāt
Kuria Muria Is.
Ra's Nawş
Dhofar
Ṣalālah
Mirbaṭ
Raysūt
Damqawt

YEMEN
Sanaa (Şan'ā')
SANAA INT'L
Jabal an Nabī Shu'ayb 3,760 m
Ma'rib
Shabwah
YEMEN
Al Ḥudaydah
Ṭa'izz
Ibb
Dhamār
Aden ('Adan)
ADEN INT'L
Zinjibār
Al Mukallā
Ḥaḑramawt
Tarīm
Shibām
Sayḥūt
Al Ghaydah
Qishn
Ra's Fartak

ARABIAN SEA

Gulf of Aden

DJIBOUTI
Djibouti

© HAMMOND WORLD ATLAS CORPORATION

Population
- ■ 2,000,000 and over
- ▣ 1,000,000 - 1,999,999
- ◉ 500,000 - 999,999
- ◎ 250,000 - 499,999
- ⊕ 100,000 - 249,999
- ⊖ 30,000 - 99,999
- ⊙ 10,000 - 29,999
- ○ Under 10,000

Land Heights
| 0 m./0 ft. | 200/700 | 500/1600 | 1000/3300 | 1500/5000 | 2000/6500 | 4000/13000 | 6000/19750 |

Ocean Depths
| 0 m./0 ft. | 200/700 | 500/1600 | 1000/3300 | 1500/5000 | 2000/6500 | 4000/13000 | 6000/19750 |

Statistics

	IRAQ	KUWAIT
AREA (sq. mi. / sq. km.):	168,753 / 437,072	6,880 / 17,820
POPULATION:	26,074,906	2,335,648
CAPITAL:	Baghdad	Kuwait
LARGEST CITY:	Baghdad	As Sālimiyah
HIGHEST POINT (m.):	(unnamed) 3,611	(unnamed) 306
GOVERNMENT TYPE:	(interim gov't)	Const. monarchy
INDEPENDENCE DATE:	Oct. 3, 1932	June 19, 1961
MAJOR LANGUAGES:	Arabic, Kurdish	Arabic
MAJOR RELIGION:	Islam	Islam
MONETARY UNIT:	New Iraqi dinar	Kuwaiti dinar
INTERNET CODE:	.iq	.kw

KUWAIT

IRAQ

Land Use, Agriculture, Livestock

DOMINANT LAND USE

- Cereals, Livestock
- Irrigated Farming
- Pasture Livestock
- Nomadic Livestock Herding
- Forests, Woodlands
- Nonproductive Land
- Urbanization

AGRICULTURE

- Barley
- Cotton
- Dates
- Rice
- Tobacco
- Vegetables
- Wheat

LIVESTOCK

- Cattle
- Goats
- Sheep

Minerals, Energy, Industry

MAJOR MINERAL RESOURCES

- (Gp) Gypsum
- (P) Phosphate
- (Na) Salt
- (S) Sulphur

ENERGY

- Major Oil Fields
- Other Oil Fields
- Natural Gas
- Oil Pipelines

INDUSTRY

- Major Industrial Areas

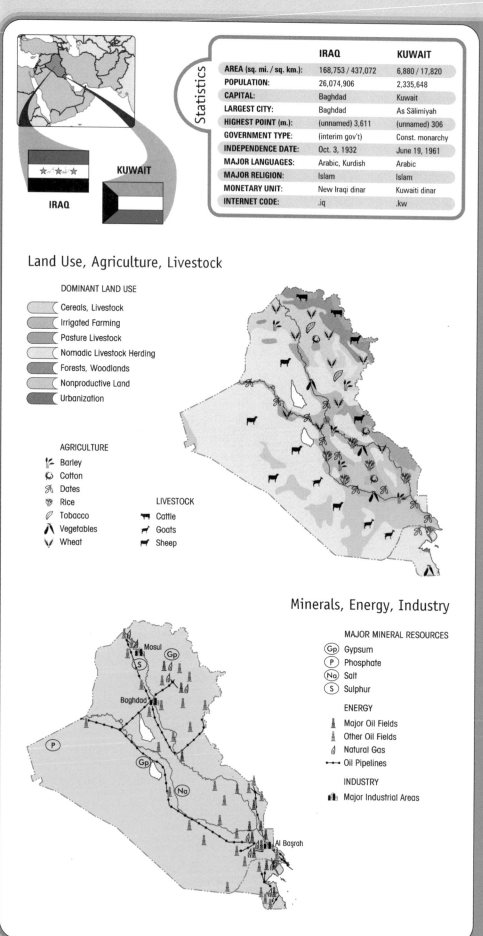

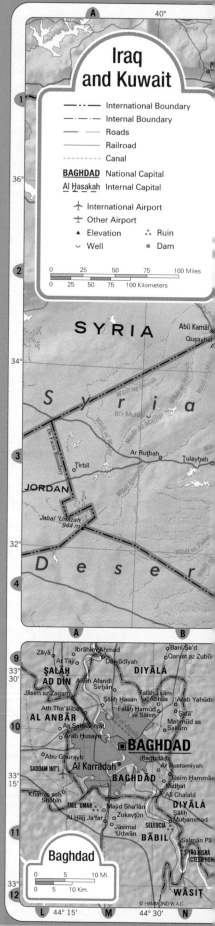

Iraq and Kuwait

- International Boundary
- Internal Boundary
- Roads
- Railroad
- Canal

BAGHDAD National Capital
Al Hasakah Internal Capital

- International Airport
- Other Airport
- Elevation
- Ruin
- Well
- Dam

0   25   50   75   100 Miles
0   25   50   75   100 Kilometers

Baghdad

0   5   10 Mi.
0   5   10 Km.

© HAMMOND W.A.C.

Kuwait (inset)

Kuwait

0   15   30 Mi.
0   15   30 Km.

Population

- ◼ 2,000,000 and over
- ⊡ 1,000,000 - 1,999,999
- ◉ 500,000 - 999,999
- ◎ 250,000 - 499,999
- ⊙ 100,000 - 249,999
- ⊙ 30,000 - 99,999
- ∘ 10,000 - 29,999
- ∘ Under 10,000

Land Heights

6000/19750   4000/13000   2000/6500   1500/5000   1000/3300   500/1600   200/700   0 m./0 ft.

Ocean Depths

0 m./0 ft.   200/700   500/1600   1000/3300   1500/5000   2000/6500   4000/13000   6000/19750

Longitude East 44° of Greenwich

© HAMMOND WORLD ATLAS CORPORATION

© HAMMOND W.A.C.

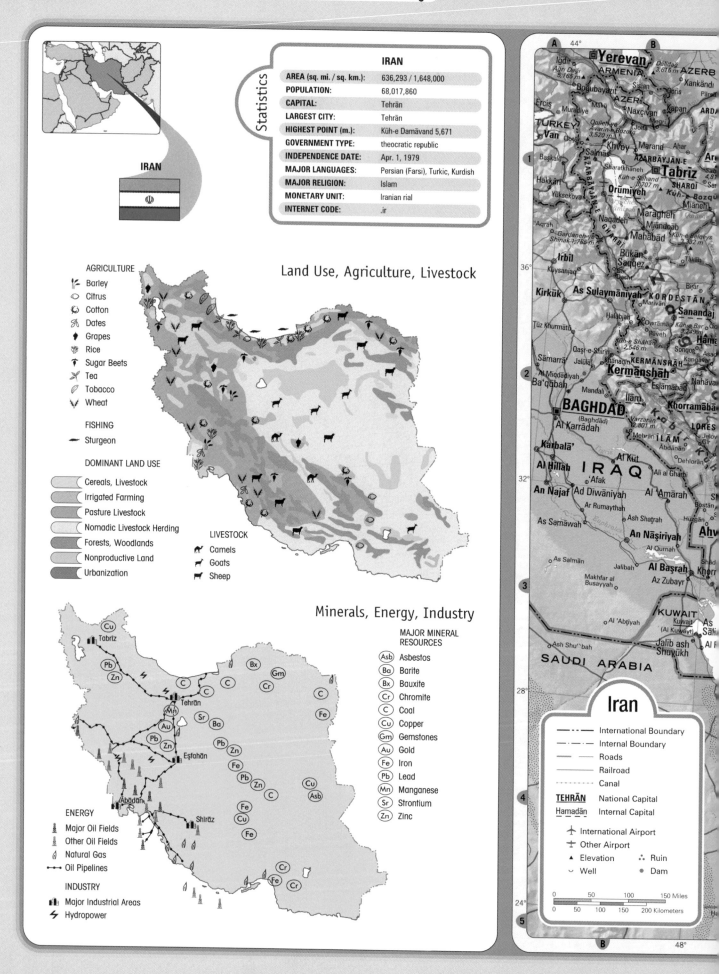

Statistics

IRAN	
AREA (sq. mi. / sq. km.):	636,293 / 1,648,000
POPULATION:	68,017,860
CAPITAL:	Tehrān
LARGEST CITY:	Tehrān
HIGHEST POINT (m.):	Kūh-e Damāvand 5,671
GOVERNMENT TYPE:	theocratic republic
INDEPENDENCE DATE:	Apr. 1, 1979
MAJOR LANGUAGES:	Persian (Farsi), Turkic, Kurdish
MAJOR RELIGION:	Islam
MONETARY UNIT:	Iranian rial
INTERNET CODE:	.ir

IRAN

Land Use, Agriculture, Livestock

AGRICULTURE
- Barley
- Citrus
- Cotton
- Dates
- Grapes
- Rice
- Sugar Beets
- Tea
- Tobacco
- Wheat

FISHING
- Sturgeon

DOMINANT LAND USE
- Cereals, Livestock
- Irrigated Farming
- Pasture Livestock
- Nomadic Livestock Herding
- Forests, Woodlands
- Nonproductive Land
- Urbanization

LIVESTOCK
- Camels
- Goats
- Sheep

Minerals, Energy, Industry

MAJOR MINERAL RESOURCES
- Asb Asbestos
- Ba Barite
- Bx Bauxite
- Cr Chromite
- C Coal
- Cu Copper
- Gm Gemstones
- Au Gold
- Fe Iron
- Pb Lead
- Mn Manganese
- Sr Strontium
- Zn Zinc

ENERGY
- Major Oil Fields
- Other Oil Fields
- Natural Gas
- Oil Pipelines

INDUSTRY
- Major Industrial Areas
- Hydropower

Tabriz, Tehrān, Eşfahān, Ābādān, Shīrāz

Iran

- International Boundary
- Internal Boundary
- Roads
- Railroad
- Canal
- **TEHRĀN** National Capital
- Hamadān Internal Capital
- International Airport
- Other Airport
- Elevation
- Well
- Ruin
- Dam

| 0 | 50 | 100 | 150 Miles |
| 0 | 50 | 100 | 150 | 200 Kilometers |

Population

■ 2,000,000 and over
▣ 1,000,000 - 1,999,999
◉ 500,000 - 999,999
◉ 250,000 - 499,999
◉ 100,000 - 249,999
◉ 30,000 - 99,999
◉ 10,000 - 29,999
○ Under 10,000

Land Heights

Ocean Depths

© HAMMOND WORLD ATLAS CORPORATION

Statistics

AFGHANISTAN

AREA (sq. mi. / sq. km.):	250,000 / 647,500
POPULATION:	29,928,987
CAPITAL:	Kabul
LARGEST CITY:	Kabul
HIGHEST POINT (m.):	Nowshāk 7,485
GOVERNMENT TYPE:	Islamic republic
INDEPENDENCE DATE:	Aug. 19, 1919
MAJOR LANGUAGES:	Dari, Pashtu, Uzbek
MAJOR RELIGION:	Islam
MONETARY UNIT:	afghani
INTERNET CODE:	.af

AFGHANISTAN

Land Use, Agriculture, Livestock

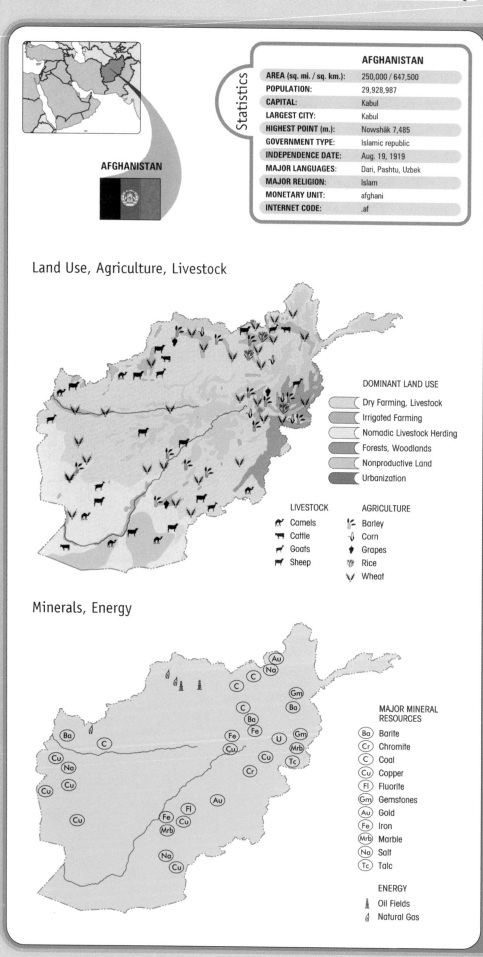

DOMINANT LAND USE
- Dry Farming, Livestock
- Irrigated Farming
- Nomadic Livestock Herding
- Forests, Woodlands
- Nonproductive Land
- Urbanization

LIVESTOCK
- Camels
- Cattle
- Goats
- Sheep

AGRICULTURE
- Barley
- Corn
- Grapes
- Rice
- Wheat

Minerals, Energy

MAJOR MINERAL RESOURCES
- (Ba) Barite
- (Cr) Chromite
- (C) Coal
- (Cu) Copper
- (Fl) Fluorite
- (Gm) Gemstones
- (Au) Gold
- (Fe) Iron
- (Mrb) Marble
- (Na) Salt
- (Tc) Talc

ENERGY
- Oil Fields
- Natural Gas

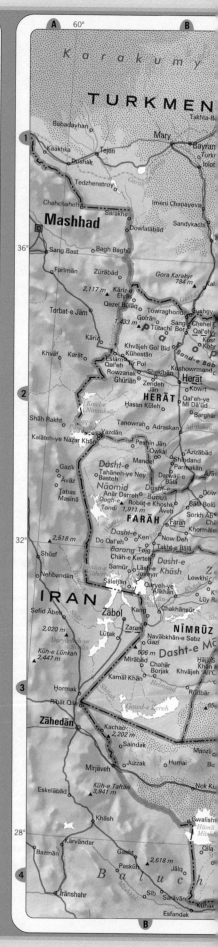

Afghanistan

Population
- ■ 2,000,000 and over
- ◻ 1,000,000 - 1,999,999
- ◉ 500,000 - 999,999
- ◎ 250,000 - 499,999
- ⊕ 100,000 - 249,999
- ⊙ 30,000 - 99,999
- ○ 10,000 - 29,999
- ○ Under 10,000

Afghanistan
- —·—··— International Boundary
- —·—·— Internal Boundary
- — — Roads
- —— Railroad
- ········ Canal
- **KABUL** National Capital
- Kandahār Internal Capital
- ✈ International Airport
- ✦ Other Airport
- ▲ Elevation
- ● Dam

0 25 50 75 100 Miles
0 25 50 75 100 Kilometers

Land Heights
0 m./ 0 ft. 200/700 500/1600 1000/3300 1500/5000 2000/6500 4000/13000 6000/19750

Ocean Depths
0 m./ 0 ft. 200/700 500/1600 1000/3300 1500/5000 2000/6500 4000/13000 6000/19750

© HAMMOND WORLD ATLAS CORPORATION

Longitude East 72° of Greenwich

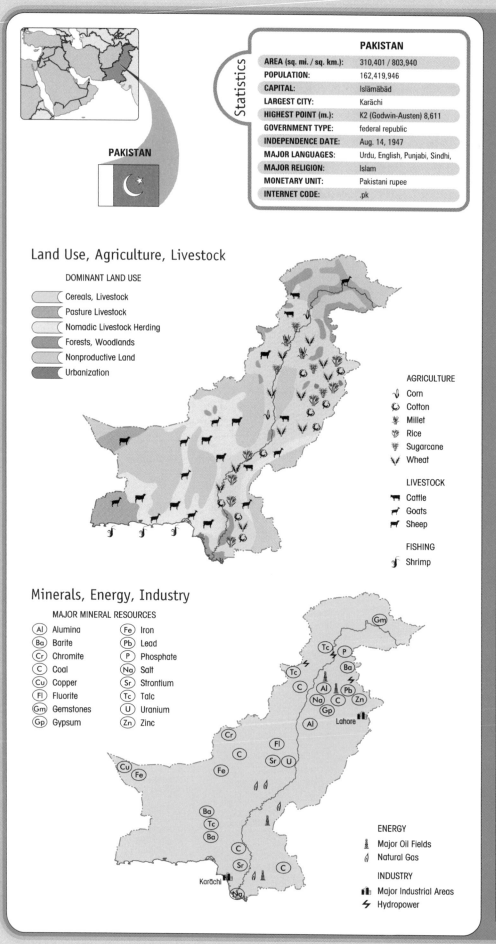

Statistics

PAKISTAN	
AREA (sq. mi. / sq. km.):	310,401 / 803,940
POPULATION:	162,419,946
CAPITAL:	Islāmābād
LARGEST CITY:	Karāchi
HIGHEST POINT (m.):	K2 (Godwin-Austen) 8,611
GOVERNMENT TYPE:	federal republic
INDEPENDENCE DATE:	Aug. 14, 1947
MAJOR LANGUAGES:	Urdu, English, Punjabi, Sindhi,
MAJOR RELIGION:	Islam
MONETARY UNIT:	Pakistani rupee
INTERNET CODE:	.pk

PAKISTAN

Land Use, Agriculture, Livestock

DOMINANT LAND USE

- Cereals, Livestock
- Pasture Livestock
- Nomadic Livestock Herding
- Forests, Woodlands
- Nonproductive Land
- Urbanization

AGRICULTURE

- Corn
- Cotton
- Millet
- Rice
- Sugarcane
- Wheat

LIVESTOCK

- Cattle
- Goats
- Sheep

FISHING

- Shrimp

Minerals, Energy, Industry

MAJOR MINERAL RESOURCES

- (Al) Alumina
- (Ba) Barite
- (Cr) Chromite
- (C) Coal
- (Cu) Copper
- (Fl) Fluorite
- (Gm) Gemstones
- (Gp) Gypsum
- (Fe) Iron
- (Pb) Lead
- (P) Phosphate
- (Na) Salt
- (Sr) Strontium
- (Tc) Talc
- (U) Uranium
- (Zn) Zinc

ENERGY

- Major Oil Fields
- Natural Gas

INDUSTRY

- Major Industrial Areas
- Hydropower

Karāchi – Hyderābād

© HAMMOND W.A.C.

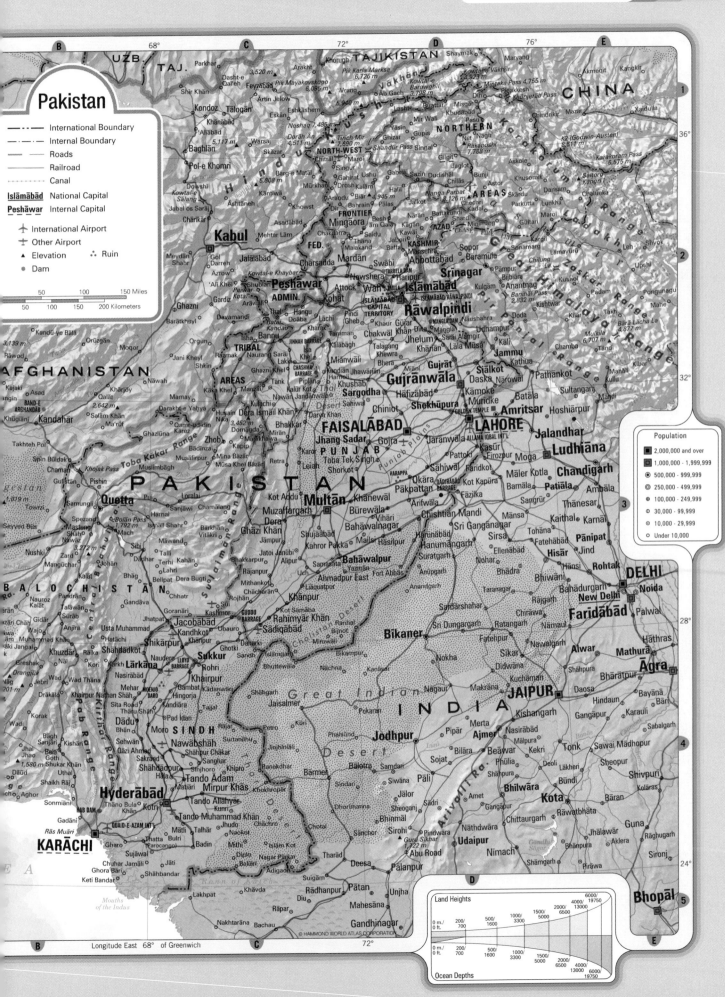

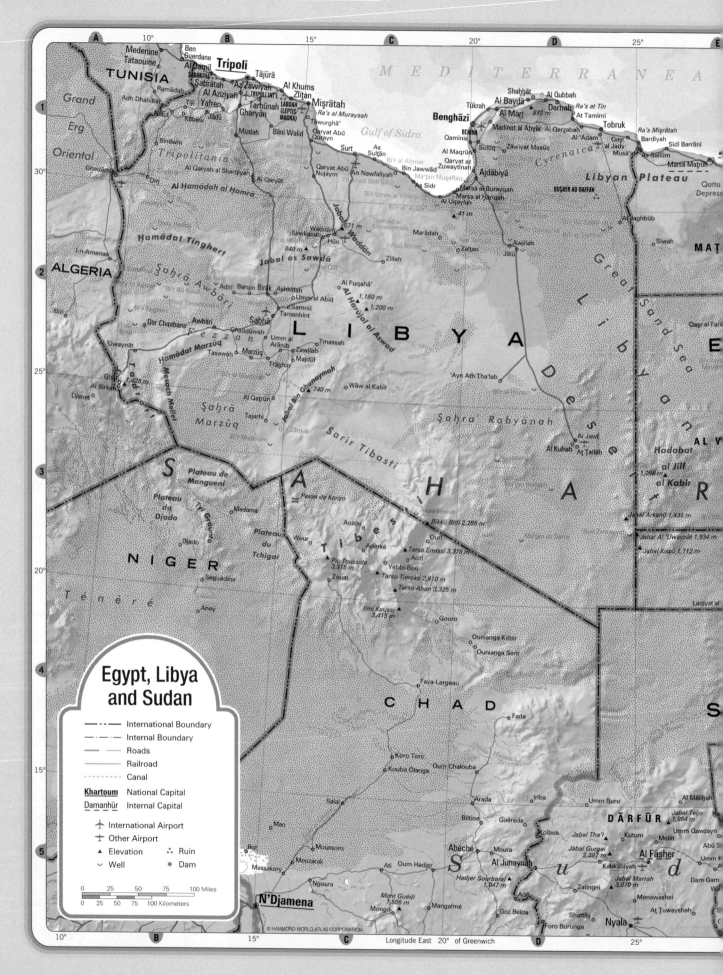

Egypt, Libya and Sudan

‒‒‒‒	International Boundary
‒‒‒‒	Internal Boundary
‒‒‒	Roads
———	Railroad
·········	Canal
Khartoum	National Capital
Damanhūr	Internal Capital
✈	International Airport
✈	Other Airport
▲ Elevation	∴ Ruin
⌣ Well	● Dam

0   25   50   75   100 Miles
0   25   50   75   100 Kilometers

© HAMMOND WORLD ATLAS CORPORATION

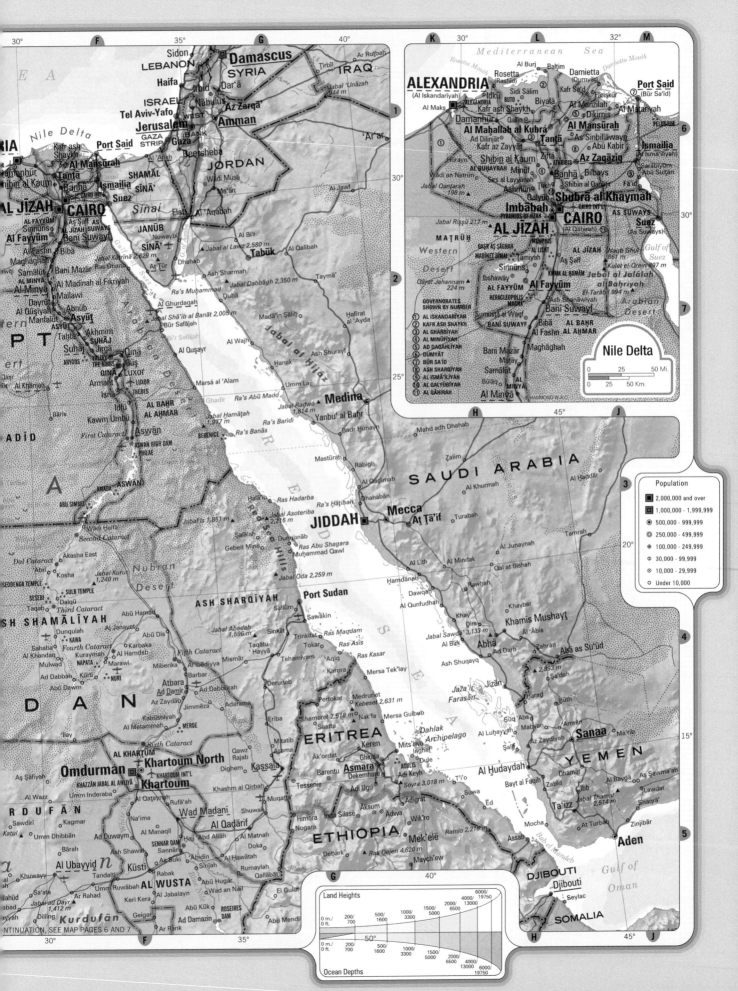

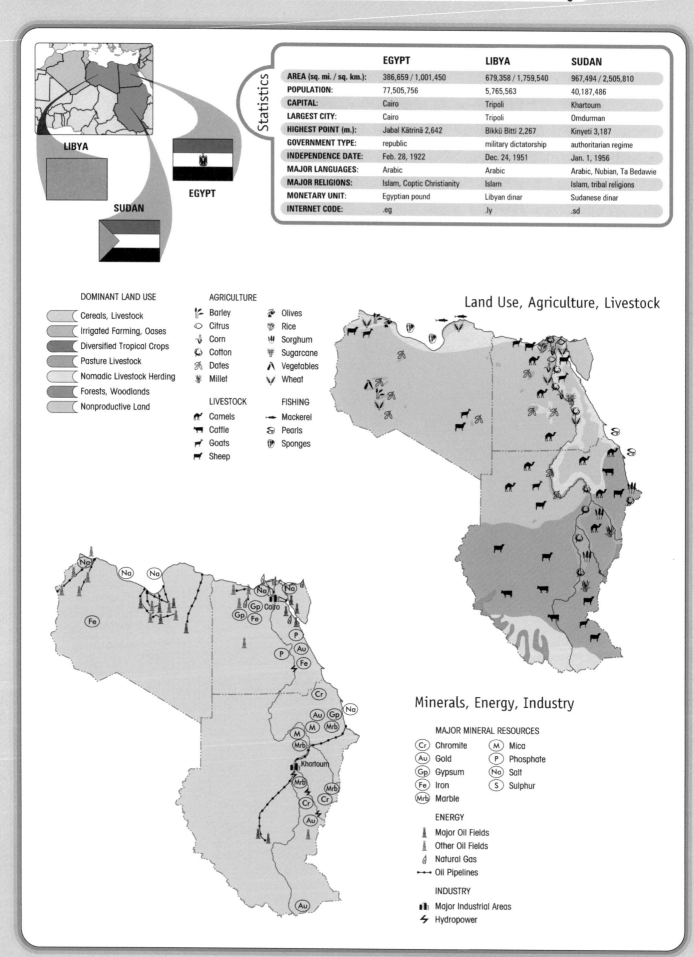

Statistics

	EGYPT	LIBYA	SUDAN
AREA (sq. mi. / sq. km.):	386,659 / 1,001,450	679,358 / 1,759,540	967,494 / 2,505,810
POPULATION:	77,505,756	5,765,563	40,187,486
CAPITAL:	Cairo	Tripoli	Khartoum
LARGEST CITY:	Cairo	Tripoli	Omdurman
HIGHEST POINT (m.):	Jabal Kātrīnā 2,642	Bikkū Bitti 2,267	Kinyeti 3,187
GOVERNMENT TYPE:	republic	military dictatorship	authoritarian regime
INDEPENDENCE DATE:	Feb. 28, 1922	Dec. 24, 1951	Jan. 1, 1956
MAJOR LANGUAGES:	Arabic	Arabic	Arabic, Nubian, Ta Bedawie
MAJOR RELIGIONS:	Islam, Coptic Christianity	Islam	Islam, tribal religions
MONETARY UNIT:	Egyptian pound	Libyan dinar	Sudanese dinar
INTERNET CODE:	.eg	.ly	.sd

LIBYA

EGYPT

SUDAN

DOMINANT LAND USE

- Cereals, Livestock
- Irrigated Farming, Oases
- Diversified Tropical Crops
- Pasture Livestock
- Nomadic Livestock Herding
- Forests, Woodlands
- Nonproductive Land

AGRICULTURE

- Barley
- Citrus
- Corn
- Cotton
- Dates
- Millet
- Olives
- Rice
- Sorghum
- Sugarcane
- Vegetables
- Wheat

LIVESTOCK

- Camels
- Cattle
- Goats
- Sheep

FISHING

- Mackerel
- Pearls
- Sponges

Land Use, Agriculture, Livestock

Minerals, Energy, Industry

MAJOR MINERAL RESOURCES

- Cr Chromite
- Au Gold
- Gp Gypsum
- Fe Iron
- Mrb Marble
- M Mica
- P Phosphate
- Na Salt
- S Sulphur

ENERGY

- Major Oil Fields
- Other Oil Fields
- Natural Gas
- Oil Pipelines

INDUSTRY

- Major Industrial Areas
- Hydropower

Cairo

Khartoum

Statistics

	ALGERIA	MOROCCO	TUNISIA
AREA (sq. mi. / sq. km.):	919,591 / 2,381,740	172,414 / 446,550	63,170, 163,610
POPULATION:	32,531,853	32,725,847	10,074,951
CAPITAL:	Algiers	Rabat	Tūnis
LARGEST CITY:	Algiers	Casablanca	Tūnis
HIGHEST POINT (m.):	Tahat 3,003	Jebel Toubkal 4,165	Jebel ech Chambi 1,544
GOVERNMENT TYPE:	republic	constitutional monarchy	republic
INDEPENDENCE DATE:	July 5, 1962	March 2, 1956	March 20, 1956
MAJOR LANGUAGES:	Arabic, Berber, French	Arabic, Berber, French	Arabic, French
MAJOR RELIGIONS:	Islam	Islam	Islam
MONETARY UNIT:	Algerian dinar	Moroccan dirham	Tunisian dinar
INTERNET CODE:	.dz	.ma	.tn

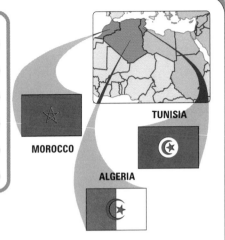

TUNISIA

MOROCCO

ALGERIA

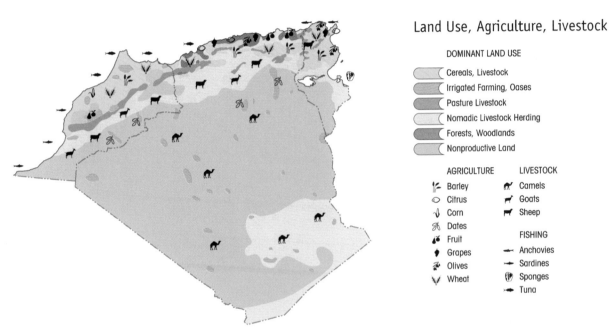

Land Use, Agriculture, Livestock

DOMINANT LAND USE

- Cereals, Livestock
- Irrigated Farming, Oases
- Pasture Livestock
- Nomadic Livestock Herding
- Forests, Woodlands
- Nonproductive Land

AGRICULTURE

- Barley
- Citrus
- Corn
- Dates
- Fruit
- Grapes
- Olives
- Wheat

LIVESTOCK

- Camels
- Goats
- Sheep

FISHING

- Anchovies
- Sardines
- Sponges
- Tuna

Minerals, Energy, Industry

MAJOR MINERAL RESOURCES

- (Sb) Antimony
- (Ba) Barite
- (C) Coal
- (Co) Cobalt
- (Cu) Copper
- (F) Fluorspar
- (Au) Gold
- (Fe) Iron
- (Pb) Lead
- (Mn) Manganese
- (P) Phosphate
- (Ag) Silver
- (Zn) Zinc

ENERGY

- Major Oil Fields
- Other Oil Fields
- Natural Gas
- Oil Pipelines

INDUSTRY

- Major Industrial Areas
- Hydropower

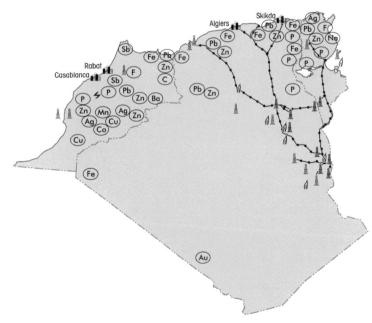

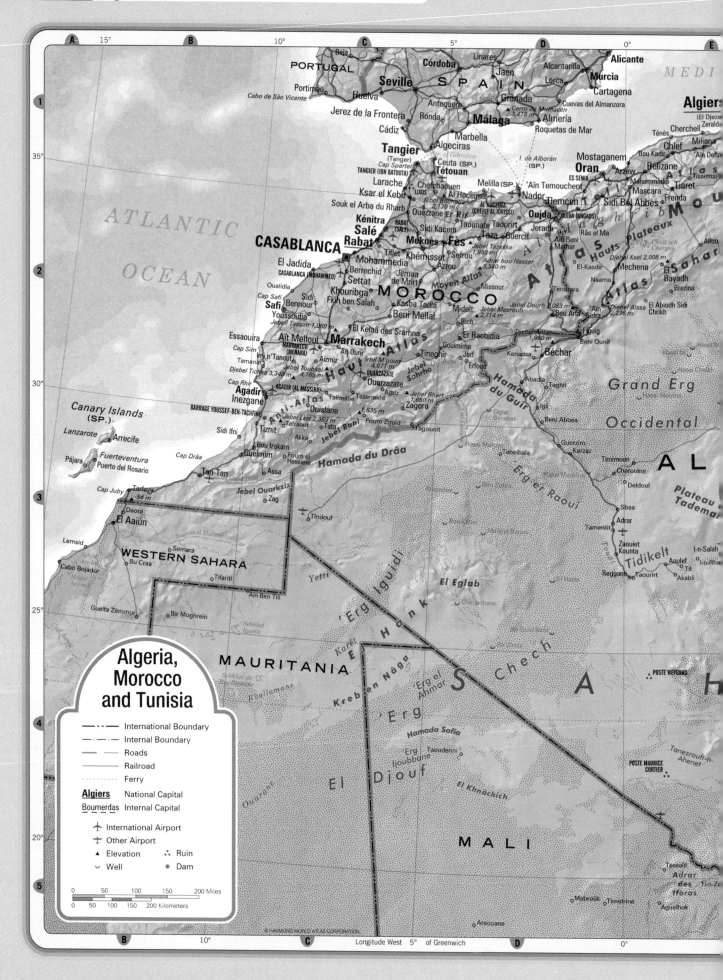

Algeria,
Morocco
and Tunisia

▬·▬·▬·	International Boundary
▬·—·▬	Internal Boundary
▬ ▬ ▬	Roads
▬▬▬	Railroad
··········	Ferry
Algiers	National Capital
Boumerdas	Internal Capital
✈	International Airport
✛	Other Airport
▲	Elevation
∴	Ruin
⌣	Well
●	Dam

Scale: 0 50 100 150 200 Miles
0 50 100 150 200 Kilometers

® HAMMOND WORLD ATLAS CORPORATION

Longitude West 5° of Greenwich

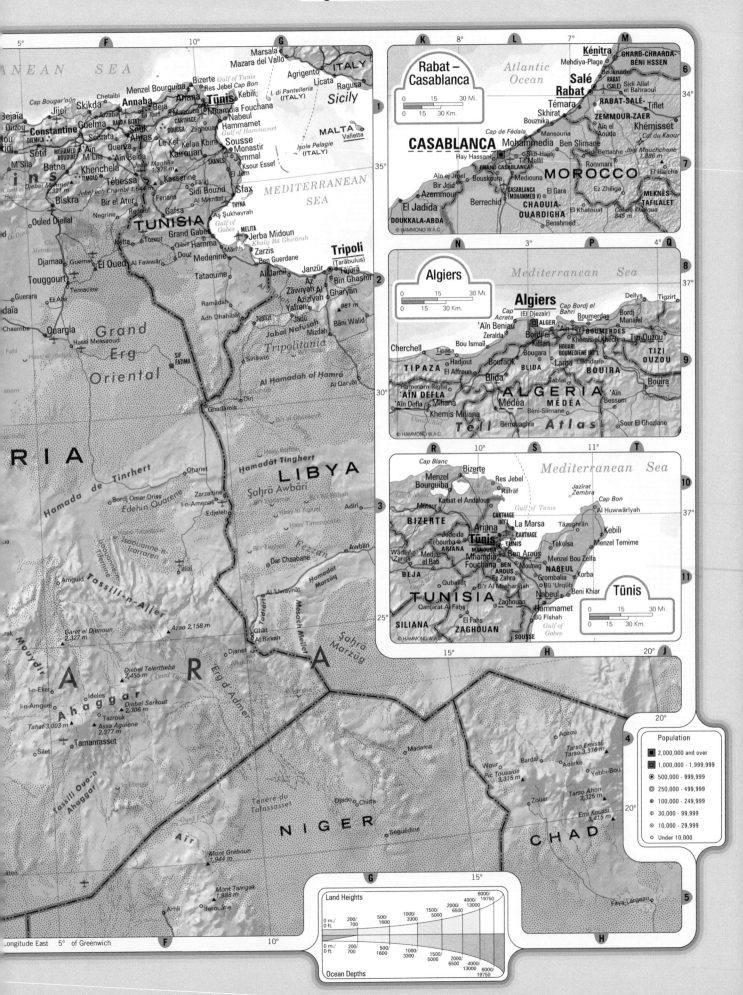

MEDITERRANEAN SEA

Inset: Rabat – Casablanca

Atlantic Ocean

0   15   30 Mi.
0   15   30 Km.

Kénitra
GHARB-CHRARDA-BÉNI HSSEN
Mehdiya-Plage
Bouknadel
Salé
RABAT (SALE)
Rabat
Sidi Allal el Bahraoui
Témara
ZEMMOUR-ZAER
Skhirat
RABAT-SALÉ-
Bouznika
'Aïn el Aouda
Khémisset
CASABLANCA
Mohammedia
Ben Slimane
Mansouria
Col du Kaour 1,086 m
Hay Hassan
Sidi-Hajjaj
Sidi Bettache
Jbel Mouchchene
Tit Mellil
Rommani
GRAND CASABLANCA
Bouskoura
MOROCCO
El Harcha
Aïn ej Jmel
Mediouna
CASABLANCA (MOHAMMED V)
Azemmour
Bir Jdid
El Gara
Ez Zhliga
Berrechid
CHAOUIA-OUARDIGHA
MEKNÈS-TAFILALET
El Jadida
DOUKKALA-ABDA
El Khatouat
Col de Khaloua 845 m
Benahmed
© HAMMOND W.A.C.

Cap de Fédala

Inset: Algiers

Mediterranean Sea

0   15   30 Mi.
0   15   30 Km.

Algiers (El Djezair)
Cap Bordj el Bahri
Dellys
Tigzirt
Cap Acrata
ALGER
Boumerdes
Bordj Manajel
'Aïn Taya
BOUMERDES
Cherchell
'Aïn Beniau
Tizi-Ouzou
Zeralda
Bordj el Kiffan
TIZI OUZOU
Tipasa
Bou Ismail
Khemis el Khechna
TIPAZA
Bougara
HOUARI BOUMEDIENE INT'L
Bouira
Hadjout
Boufarik
Larba
Lakhdaria
BOUIRA
El Affroun
BLIDA
Bouira
'AÏN DEFLA
Blida
Tablat
Hammam-Righa
Aïn Defla
Médéa
MÉDÉA
'Aïn Bessem
Miliana
ALGERIA
Khemis Miliana
Béni-Slimane
Sour El Ghozlane
Berrouaghia
Tell   Atlas
© HAMMOND W.A.C.

Inset: Tūnis

Mediterranean Sea

Cap Blanc
Bizerte
Res Jebel
Jazirat Zembra
Menzel Bourguiba
Kaleat el Andalous
Rafraf
Cap Bon
Mateur
Gulf of Tunis
Al Huwwārīyah
BIZERTE
Ariana
CARTHAGE INT'L
Wādī az-Zarqa
Jedeida
La Marsa
Tāzughrān
Tebourba
CARTHAGE
Kebili
Medjez el Bab
ARIANA
Tūnis
TŪNIS
Takelsa
MANOUBA
Menzel Temime
BEJA
Mhamdia Fouchana
BEN AROUS
Menzel Bou Zelfa
Ben Arous
Mounag
Korba
Ez Zahra
Grombalia
Quballat
NABEUL
Bū 'Urqūb
Beni Khiar
Bir Al Mashariqah
Nabeul
Tūnis
SILIANA
Qantarat Al Fahs
Zaghouan
Hammamet
0   15   30 Mi.
El Fahs
ZAGHOUAN
Bū Fishah
Gulf of Gabes
0   15   30 Km.
TUNISIA
SOUSSE
© HAMMOND W.A.C.

Marsala
Mazara del Vallo
Agrigento
ITALY
Bizerte
Gulf of Tunis
Res Jebel Cap Bon
Chetaibi
I. di Pantelleria (ITALY)
Licata
Ragusa
Sicily
Menzel Bourguiba
Annaba
Ariana
Tūnis
Skikda
MALTA
Valletta
Jijel
Azzaba
El Tarf
Mhamdia Fouchana
Guelma
RABH BIJAT
La Manouba
Nabeul
Bejaïa
Ouzou
Constantine
Souk Ahras
Béja
DOUGGA
CARTHAGE
Zaghouan
Hammamet
Isole Pelagie (ITALY)
DJEMILA
Sedrata
Querza
Le Kef
Kelaa Kbira
Sousse
MEDITERRANEAN SEA
Setif
MOHAMED BOUDIAF
'Aïn Beida
Kairouan
Monastir
M'Sila
Batna
'Aïn M'Lila
SKANES
ins
Khenchela
Jabal Maghila 1,378 m
Jemmal
Ksour Essef
Djebel Mrehel 2,321 m
TIMGAD
Tébessa
Kasserine
El Jem
Jebel ech Chambi 1,544 m
Sfax
Biskra
Fa'id
Sidi Bouzid
Chott el Hodna
Feriana
Al Miknasi
Ouled Djellal
Redeief
Aş Şukhayrah
Négrine
Gafsa
Nefta
TUNISIA
Gulf of Gabes
Chott Meroane
Tozeur
Grand Gabes
MELITA
Jerba Midoun
Djamaa
Guemar
Qibili Hamma
Khalij Bū Ghirārah
El Oued
Al Fawwār
Douz
Zarzis
Touggourt
Medenine
Tripoli
Temacine
Mareth
Ben Guerdane
(Tarābulus)
Guerara
'Ala
Hassi Messaoud
Tataouine
Al Jamil
Tajūra
daïa
Chaamba
Ramadah
Az Zāwiyah Al
Janzūr
Bir Ghashīr
Grand
Fahl
Hassi r'Mel
Adh Dhahibat
Aziziyah
Gharyān
Ouargla
Erg
Nalut
Yafran
Jadu
981 m
Bāni Walid
Oriental
Jabal Nafusah
Mizdah
anem
SIF FATIMA
Sinawin
Tripolitania
Ghadāmis
Dirj
Al Hamadah al Hamra
Al Qaryāt
RIA
LIBYA
Hamadāt Tinrhert
Hamada de Tinrhert
Ohanet
Bir el Ghanam
Hamadāt Marzūq
Bordj Omar Driss
Zarzaitine
Sahra Awbari
Edehin Ouarene
I-n-Amenas
Hasy el Ajram
Adiri
Edjeleh
Hasy Timenoua
Awbari
Isaouanne-n-Irrarraren
Bir Zgaiten
Fezzan
Dar Chaabane
Ghat
Amguid
Tiliui
Hamadāt Marzūq
Tassili-n-Ajjer
Garet el Djenoun 2,327 m
Azao 2,158 m
Mesach Mellet
Sahra Marzūg
Moydir
Ghat
Sahra Marzuq
Djanet
Ahaggar
Al Birkah
Alkomn
A   R   A
I-n-Eker
Djebel Teltheba 2,455 m
Oued Tan
Idéles
Djebel Serkout 2,306 m
I-n-Amguel
Tazrouk
Erg d'Admer
Tahat 3,003 m
Assa Aguiène 2,377 m
Silet
Tamanrasset
Madama
Aozou
Tarso Emissi Tarso 3,376 m
Tassili Oua-n-Ahaggar
Wour
Bardai
Aderke
Yebbi-Bou
Tassili Oua-n-Ahaggar
Pic Tousside 3,315 m
Tibesti
N I G E R
Tenéré du Tafassasset
Djado
Chirfa
Zouar
Tarso Ahon 3,325 m
Emi Koussi 3,415 m
CHAD
Air
Séguédine
Mont Gréboun 1,944 m
Arhli
Mont Tamgak 1,988 m
Iferouane
Faya-Largeau

Population

■ 2,000,000 and over
▣ 1,000,000 - 1,999,999
● 500,000 - 999,999
◉ 250,000 - 499,999
⊕ 100,000 - 249,999
⊘ 30,000 - 99,999
⊙ 10,000 - 29,999
○ Under 10,000

Land Heights

0 m./ 0 ft.
200/ 700
500/ 1600
1000/ 3300
1500/ 5000
2000/ 6500
4000/ 13000
6000/ 19750

Ocean Depths

0 m./ 0 ft.
200/ 700
500/ 1600
1000/ 3300
2000/ 6500
4000/ 13000
6000/ 19750

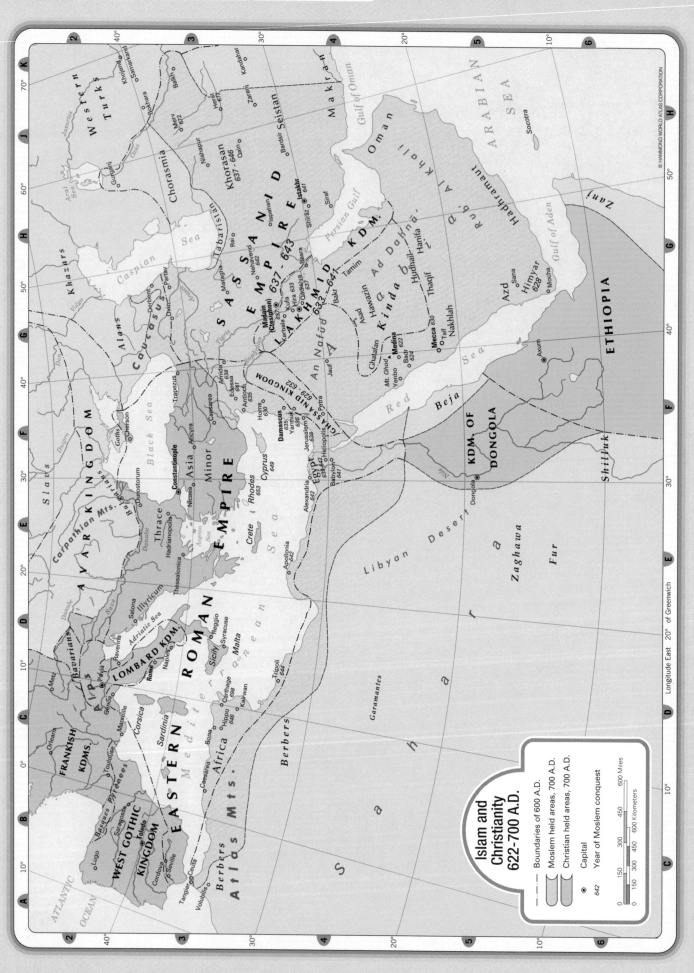

Based on the "Atlas of Islamic History" by Harry W. Hazard, by permission of Princeton University Press.

Islam and
Christianity
622-700 A.D.

— · — · —　Boundaries of 600 A.D.

Moslem held areas, 700 A.D.

Christian held areas, 700 A.D.

⊙　Capital

642　Year of Moslem conquest

| 0 | 150 | 300 | 450 | 600 Miles |

| 0 | 150 | 300 | 450 | 600 Kilometers |

© HAMMOND WORLD ATLAS CORPORATION

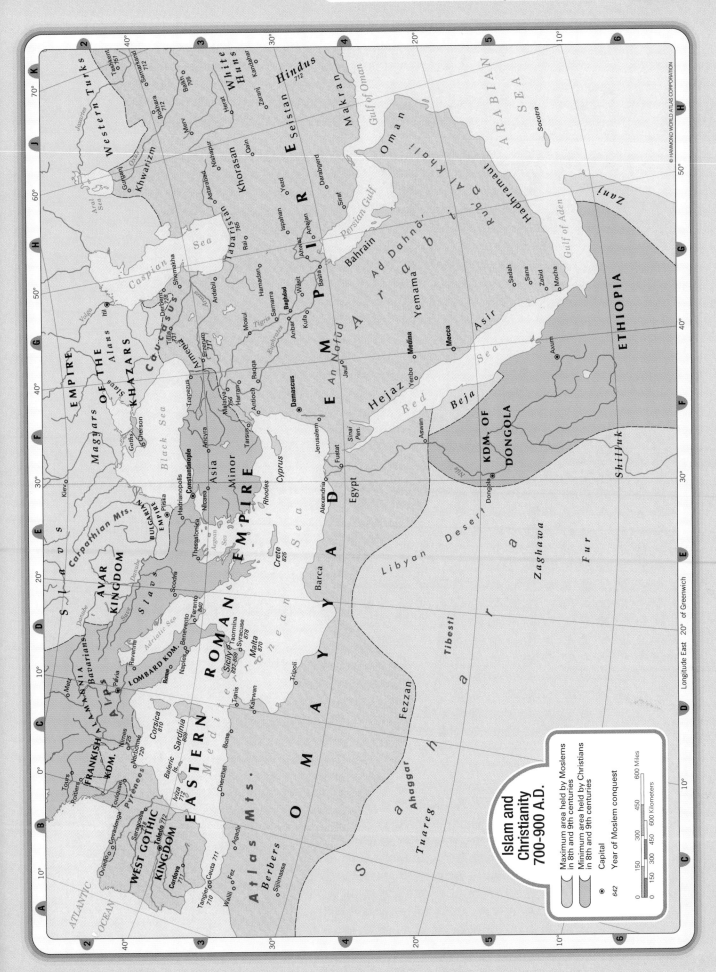

Islam and Christianity 700-900 A.D.

Maximum area held by Moslems in 8th and 9th centuries

Minimum area held by Christians in 8th and 9th centuries

⊙ Capital

642 Year of Moslem conquest

0   150   300   450   600 Miles

0   150   300   450   600 Kilometers

Western Turks

White Huns

Hindus 712

Tashkent 751

Samarkand 712

Bokhara 712

Balkh 705

Herat

Merv

Khwarizm

Gurganj

Nishapur

Astarabad

E Seistan

Makran

Khorasan

Zaranj

Kandahar

Zareh

Gulf of Oman

Oman

ARABIAN SEA

Socotra

Rai

Tabaristan

Ispahan

Yezd

Arrajan

Darabgerd

Siraf

P E R S I A

Caspian Sea

Volga

Itil

Derbent 728

Shemakha

Ardebil

Hamadan

Ahwaz

Persian Gulf

Bahrain

Ad Dahnā

Rub' Al Khali

Hadhramaut

Zanj

Caucasus

Tiflis 731

Armenia

Erzerum 717

Mosul

Samarra

Baghdad

Wasit

Basra

Kufa

Anbar

Tigris

Euphrates

Y E M A M A

Asir

Sadah

Sana

Zabid

Mocha

MAGYARS OF THE

Alans

Slavs

KHAZARS

EMPIRE

Trapezus

Raqqa

Harran

Antioch

An Nafud

Medina

Mecca

Jauf

Yenbo

Red Sea

Beja

Axum

ETHIOPIA

Kiev

Goths

Cherson

Black Sea

Malatya 756

Tarsus

Damascus

Hejaz

Yenbo

Shilluk

Constantinople

Hadrianopolis

Pliska

Nicaea

Asia Minor

Ancyra

Cyprus

Jerusalem

Fustat

Alexandria

Egypt

Aswan

Dongola

KDM. OF DONGOLA

Zaghawa

Fur

BULGARIAN EMPIRE

Thessalonica

Aegean Sea

Rhodes

Crete 825

Barca

Libyan Desert

Tibesti

S l a v s

Carpathian Mts.

AVAR KINGDOM

Danube

Scodra

Benevento

Taranto

Syracuse 878

Malta 870

Tripoli

Fezzan

Ahaggar

Tuareg

Sahara

Alps

Bavarians

Ravenna

Pavia

LOMBARD KDM.

Naples

Rome

Sicily 827-869

Taormina 902

Tunis

Kairwan

FRANKISH ALAMANNIA

KDM.

Metz

Corsica 810

Sardinia 809

Baleric Isls.

Ivza 712

Bona

Cherchel

Atlas Mts.

Berbers

EASTERN ROMAN EMPIRE

O M A Y Y A D

Mediterranean Sea

Tours

Poitiers

Narbonne 720

Nîmes 725

Pyrénees

WEST GOTHIC KINGDOM

Oviedo

Covadonga

Saragossa 713

Toledo 712

Cordova 711

Tangier 710

Ceuta 711

Fez

Agadir

Walili

Sijilmassa

ATLANTIC OCEAN

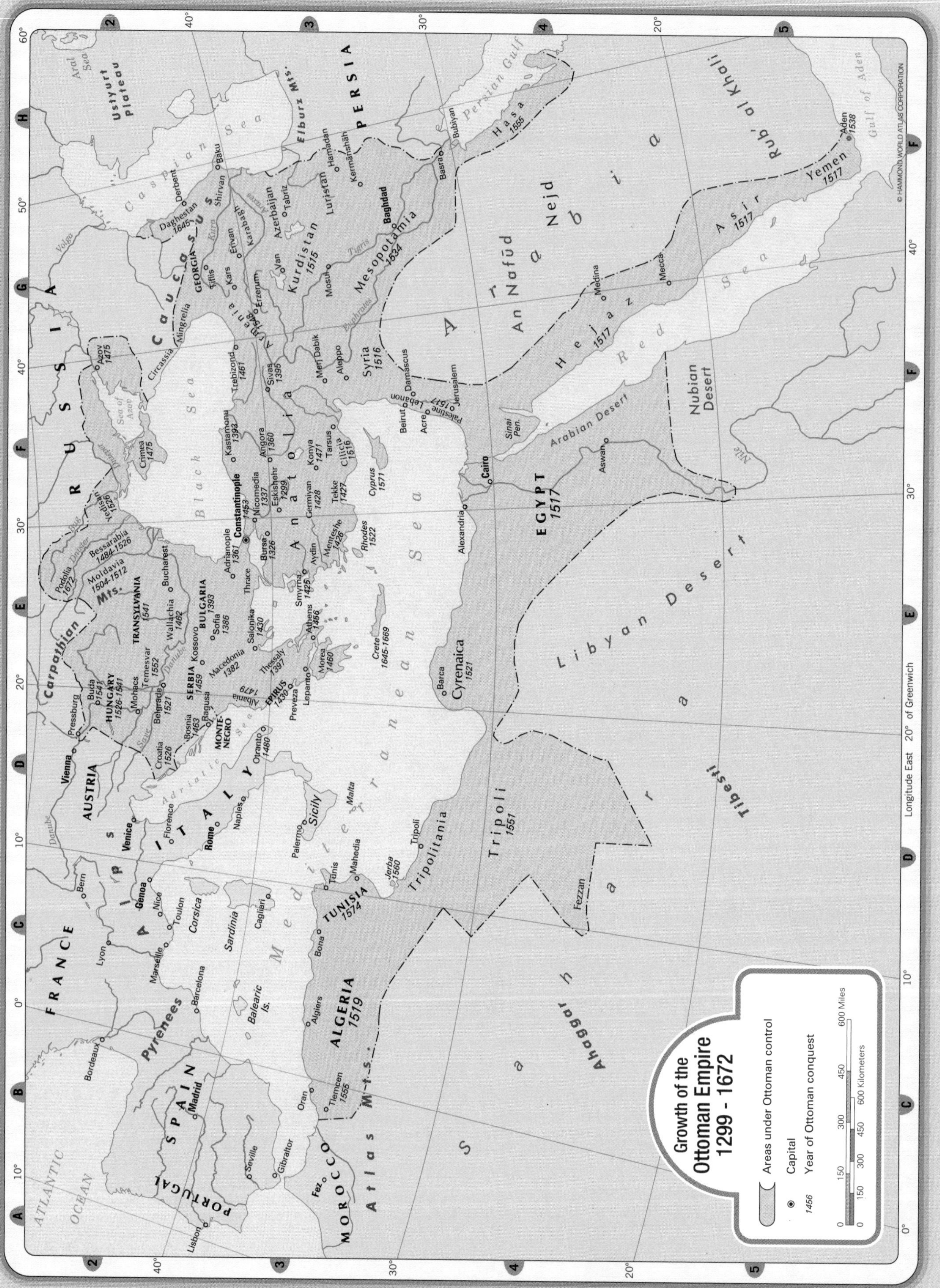

Growth of the Ottoman Empire 1299 - 1672

Legend:
- Areas under Ottoman control
- ◉ Capital
- 1456 Year of Ottoman conquest

Scale:
0 150 300 450 600 Miles
0 150 300 450 600 Kilometers

ATLANTIC OCEAN

PORTUGAL
Lisbon
SPAIN
Madrid
Seville
Gibraltar
Bordeaux
Barcelona
Oran
Tlemcen 1555
MOROCCO
Fez 1556
Atlas Mts.
Ahaggar
Sahara

FRANCE
Lyon
Marseille
Toulon
Nice
Bern
Genoa
Corsica
Sardinia
Cagliari
Balearic Is.
Algiers
ALGERIA 1519
Bona
TUNISIA 1574
Tunis
Mahedia
Jerba 1560
Tripoli
Tripolitania
Tripoli 1551

Alps
Venice
ITALY
Florence
Rome
Naples
Palermo
Sicily
Malta
Adriatic Sea
AUSTRIA
Vienna
Pressburg
Buda 1541
HUNGARY 1526-1541
Mohács
Temesvar 1552
TRANSYLVANIA 1541
Wallachia 1462
Belgrade 1521
Croatia 1526
Bosnia 1463
SERBIA 1459
Ragusa
MONTE-NEGRO
Otranto 1480
Macedonia 1382
Kossovo 1389
ALBANIA 1479
EPIRUS 1430
Preveza
Lepanto
Morea 1460
Athens 1456
Thessaly 1397
BULGARIA 1393
Sofia 1386
Salonika 1430
Thrace
Adrianople 1361
Mediterranean Sea

Carpathian Mts.
Danube
Podolia 1672
Dniester
Bessarabia 1484-1526
Moldavia 1504-1512
Bucharest
Yedisan 1526
RUSSIA
Dnieper
Don
Crimea 1475
Azov 1475
Sea of Azov
Circassia
Mingrelia
Black Sea
Ustyurt Plateau
Aral Sea
Volga
Caspian Sea

Constantinople 1453
Nicomedia 1337
Bursa 1326
Smyrna 1425
Aydin
Menteshe 1426
Rhodes 1522
Crete 1645-1669
Tekke 1427
Germian 1428
Eskishehr 1299
Angora 1360
Konya 1477
Tarsus
Cilicia 1516
Anatolia
Kastamonu 1393
Sivas 1395
Trebizond 1461
Cyprus 1571

Daghestan 1645
Derbent
Baku
Shirvan
Tiflis
GEORGIA
CAUCASUS
Kara
Karabagh
Erivan
Kars
Erzerum
Van
Armenia
Euphrates
Tigris
KURDISTAN 1515
Mosul
Azerbaijan
Tabriz
Luristan
Hamadan
Kermanshah
Baghdad 1534
Mesopotamia 1534
PERSIA
Elburz Mts.

ELBURZ MTS.
Persian Gulf
Hasa 1655
Basra
Bubiyan
An Nafud
Arabia
Nejd
Hejaz 1517
Asir 1517
Yemen 1517
Aden 1538
Gulf of Aden
Rub' al Khali
Red Sea
Mecca
Medina
Arabian Desert

Mert Dabik
Aleppo
Syria 1516
Damascus
Lebanon 1517
Beirut
Acre
Palestine 1517
Jerusalem
Sinai Pen.
Cairo
EGYPT 1517
Alexandria
Aswan
Nile
Nubian Desert
Libyan Desert
Barca
Cyrenaica 1521
Tibesti
Fezzan

Longitude East 20° of Greenwich

Based on the "Atlas of Islamic History", by Harry W. Hazard, by permission of Princeton University Press.

© HAMMOND WORLD ATLAS CORPORATION

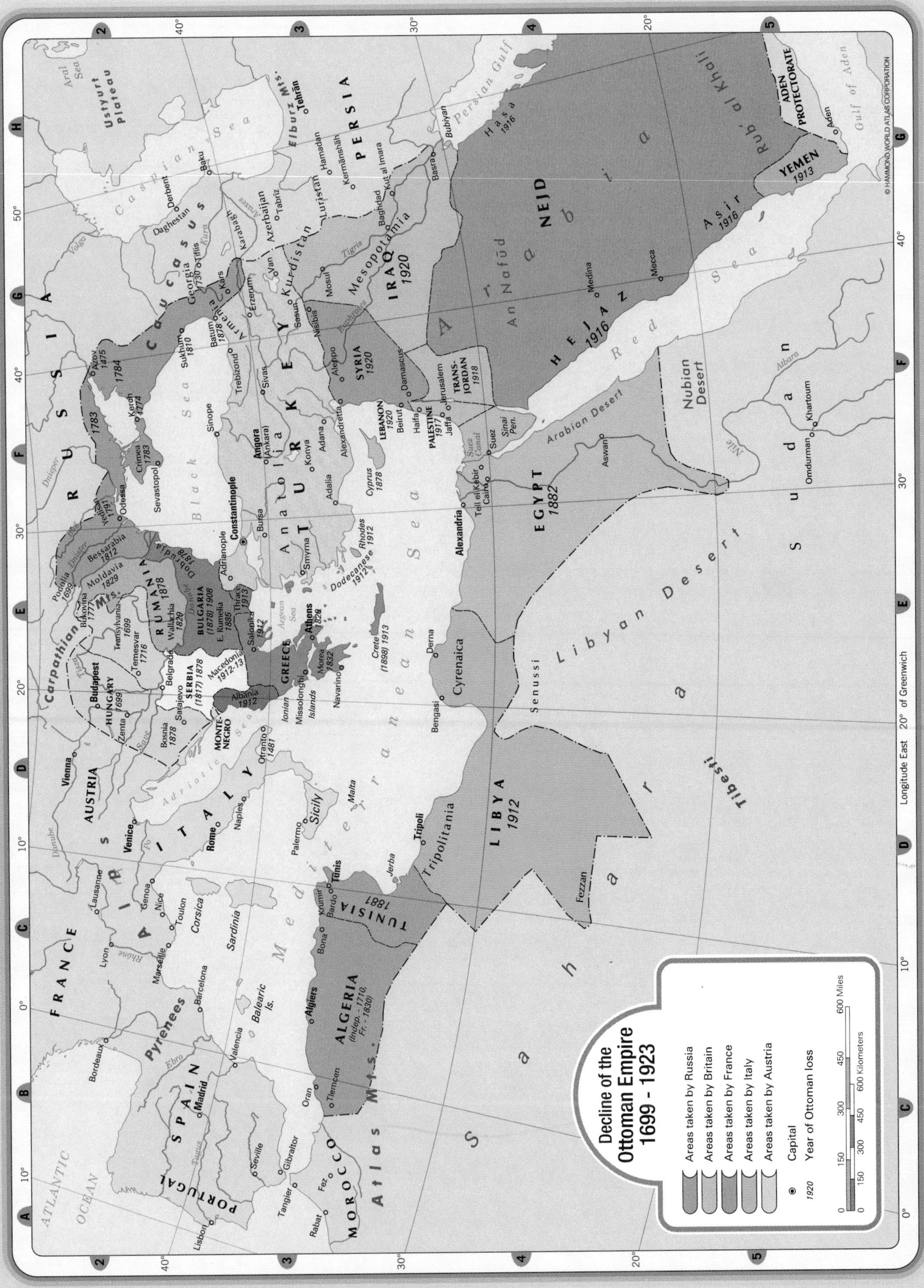

Decline of the Ottoman Empire 1699 - 1923

- Areas taken by Russia
- Areas taken by Britain
- Areas taken by France
- Areas taken by Italy
- Areas taken by Austria
- ◉ Capital
- *1920* Year of Ottoman loss

600 Miles
150 300 450 600 Kilometers
0 150 300 450 600

Longitude East 20° of Greenwich

© HAMMOND WORLD ATLAS CORPORATION

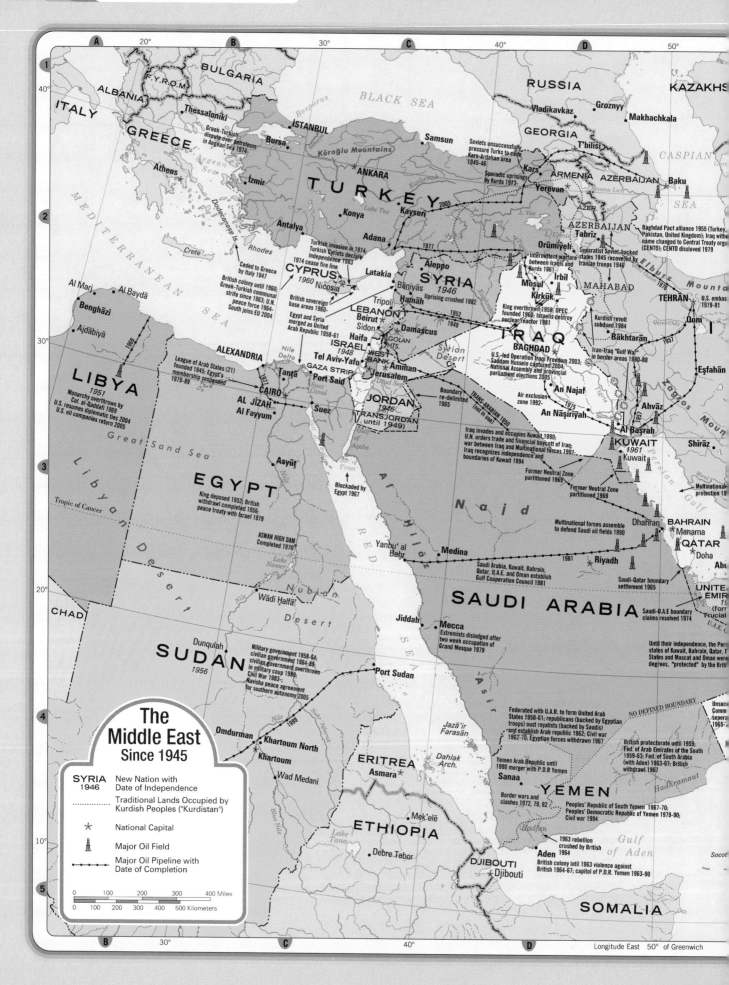

The Middle East Since 1945

SYRIA
1946   New Nation with Date of Independence

⋯⋯⋯⋯   Traditional Lands Occupied by Kurdish Peoples ("Kurdistan")

★   National Capital

⛏   Major Oil Field

•─•─•   Major Oil Pipeline with Date of Completion

0   100   200   300   400 Miles
0 100 200 300 400 500 Kilometers

Labels and annotations on map:

ITALY
ALBANIA
BULGARIA
F.Y.R.O.M.
GREECE
Thessaloniki
Athens
Izmir
Aegean Sea
Crete
Rhodes
Dodecanese Is.
MEDITERRANEAN SEA

Greek-Turkish dispute over petroleum in Aegean Sea 1974

ISTANBUL
Bursa
Bosporus
BLACK SEA
Köroğlu Mountains
ANKARA
Konya
Antalya
Adana
Kayseri
Lake Tuz
Kızılırmak
TURKEY

RUSSIA
Vladikavkaz
Groznyy
Makhachkala
GEORGIA
T'bilisi
Kars
ARMENIA
Yerevan
AZERBAIJAN
Baku
AZER.
CASPIAN SEA
KAZAKHS

Soviets unsuccessfully pressure Turks to cede Kars-Ardahan area 1945-46

Sporadic uprisings by Kurds 1973

2005
1977

Turkish invasion in 1974; Turkish Cypriots declare independence 1983
1974 cease fire line

CYPRUS
1960 Nicosia
Ceded to Greece by Italy 1947

British colony until 1960; Greek-Turkish communal strife since 1963; U.N. peace force 1964; South joins EU 2004

British sovereign base areas 1960.

Latakia
Baniyas
Tripoli
Hamah
Aleppo
SYRIA
1946
Uprising crushed 1982

Tabriz
Orūmīyeh
MAHABAD
Separatist Soviet-backed states 1945 recovered by Iranian troops 1946

Baghdad Pact alliance 1955 (Turkey, Pakistan, United Kingdom); Iraq then name changed to Central Treaty orga (CENTO); CENTO dissolved 1979

Intermittent warfare between Iraqis and Kurds 1961

Mosul
Irbil
Kirkūk
King overthrown 1958; OPEC founded 1960; Israelis destroy nuclear reactor 1981

Kurdish revolt subdued 1984

TEHRĀN
U.S. embas 1979-81
Qom
Elburz Mountains
Qareh Chāy

1978

Egypt and Syria merged as United Arab Republic 1958-61

LEBANON
Beirut
Sidon
Damascus
1952
1949
GOLAN HTS.
Syrian Desert

IRAQ
BAGHDAD
U.S.-led Operation Iraqi Freedom 2003; Saddam Hussein captured 2004; National Assembly and provincial parliament elections 2005

Haifa
ISRAEL
1948
Tel Aviv-Yafo
WEST BANK
Jerusalem
Amman
GAZA STRIP

Nile Delta
ALEXANDRIA
Tanta
Port Said
CAIRO
AL JĪZAH
AL FAYYUM
Suez Canal
Suez

League of Arab States (21) founded 1945; Egypt's membership suspended 1979-89

JORDAN
1946
(TRANSJORDAN until 1949)

Boundary re-delimited 1965

TRANS-ARABIAN 1950 (not in use)

Air exclusion zone 1992-

An Najaf
An Nāşirīyah
Iran-Iraq "Gulf War" in border areas 1980-88
Bākhtarān
1957
Eşfahān
Ahvāz
Zagros Moun
1975
1957

Iraq invades and occupies Kuwait 1990; U.N. orders trade and financial boycott of Iraq; war between Iraq and Multinational forces 1991; Iraq recognizes independence and boundaries of Kuwait 1994

Al Başrah
KUWAIT
1961
Kuwait
Shīrāz

Former Neutral Zone partitioned 1969
Former Neutral Zone partitioned 1969

Multinational protection 19

AL JIZAH
Al Marj
Al Baydā
Benghāzi
Ajdābiyā
1969
Great Sand Sea
Libyan Desert
Tropic of Cancer

LIBYA
1951
Monarchy overthrown by Col. al-Qaddafi 1969; U.S. resumes diplomatic ties 2004; U.S. oil companies return 2005

EGYPT
King deposed 1952; British withdrawl completed 1956; peace treaty with Israel 1979

ASWAN HIGH DAM Completed 1970
Lake Nasser

Asyūţ
Nile

Blockaded by Egypt 1967
Str. of Tiran
Gulf of Aqaba

Al Hijaz
RED SEA

Najd

SAUDI ARABIA

Multinational forces assemble to defend Saudi oil fields 1990
Dhahran
BAHRAIN
Manama
QATAR
Doha
Abu

Saudi-Qatar boundary settlement 1965
Riyadh
1981
Medina
Yanbu' al Bahr

Saudi Arabia, Kuwait, Bahrain, Qatar, U.A.E. and Oman establish Gulf Cooperation Council 1981

UNITE EMIR
Saudi-U.A.E boundary claims resolved 1974
U.A.E.

Until their independence, the Per states of Kuwait, Bahrain, Qatar, T States and Muscat and Oman degrees, "protected" by the Briti

CHAD
Wādī Halfā
Nile
Dunqulah
Nubian Desert

SUDAN
1956

Military government 1958-64; civilian government 1964-89; civilian government overthrown in military coup 1989; Civil War 1983-; Navisha peace agreement for southern autonomy 2005

Omdurman
Khartoum North
Khartoum
1999
Wad Medanī
Blue Nile
Nahr 'Atbarah

Jiddah
Mecca
Extremists dislodged after two week occupation of Grand Mosque 1979

Port Sudan

Jazā'ir Farasān
Dahlak Arch.
ERITREA
Asmara

NO DEFINED BOUNDARY

Federated with U.A.R. to form United Arab States 1958-61; republicans (backed by Egyptian troops) oust royalists (backed by Saudis) and establish Arab republic 1962; Civil war 1962-70; Egyptian forces withdrawn 1967

Yemen Arab Republic until 1990 merger with P.D.R. Yemen

British protectorate until 1959; Fed. of Arab Emirates of the South 1959-63; Fed. of South Arabia (with Aden) 1963-67; British withdrawl 1967

Unsuc Comm separa 1965-

Sanaa
YEMEN
Border wars and clashes 1972, 79, 82
Peoples' Republic of South Yemen 1967-70; Peoples' Democratic Republic of Yemen 1979-90; Civil war 1994

Hadhramaut

Mek'elē
ETHIOPIA
Lake Tana
Debre Tabor

1963 rebellion crushed by British 1964

Radfan

Aden
British colony until 1963 violence against British 1964-67; capitol of P.D.R. Yemen 1963-90

Gulf of Aden
Socot

DJIBOUTI
Djibouti

SOMALIA

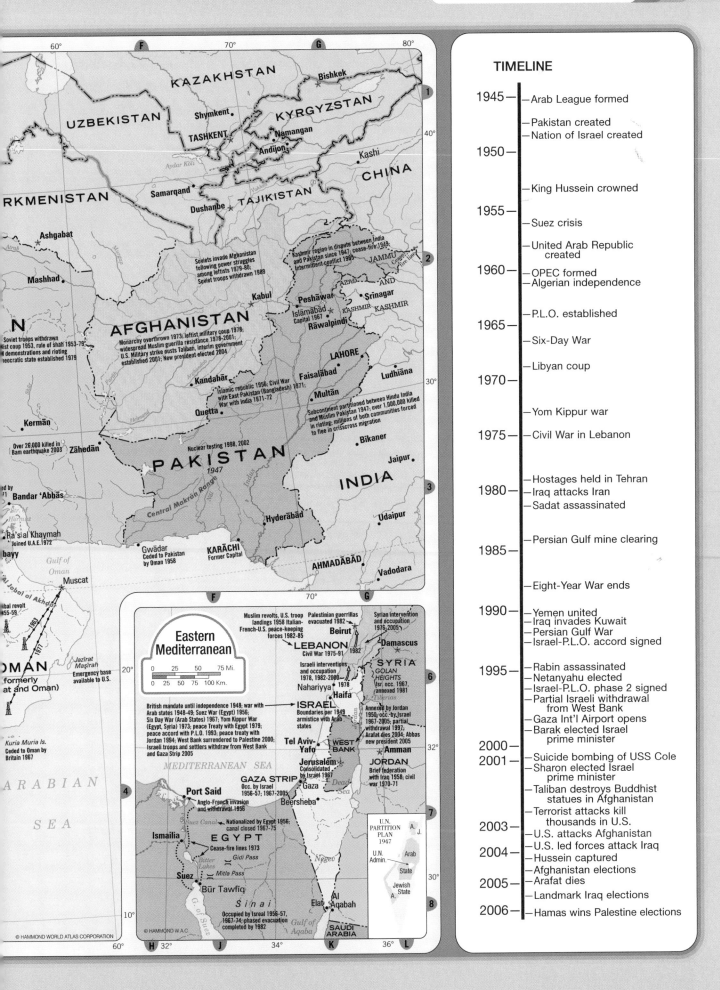

Eastern Mediterranean

0   25   50   75 Mi.
0   25   50   75   100 Km.

British mandate until independence 1948; war with
Arab states 1948–49; Suez War (Egypt) 1956;
Six Day War (Arab States) 1967; Yom Kippur War
(Egypt, Syria) 1973; peace Treaty with Egypt 1979;
peace accord with P.L.O. 1993; peace treaty with
Jordan 1994; West Bank surrendered to Palestine 2000;
Israeli troops and settlers withdraw from West Bank
and Gaza Strip 2005

Muslim revolts, U.S. troop
landings 1958 Italian-
French-U.S. peace-keeping
forces 1982–85

Palestinian guerrillas
evacuated 1982

Syrian intervention
and occupation
1976–2005

Beirut

LEBANON
Civil War 1975–91

Damascus

Israeli interventions
and occupation
1978, 1982–2000

SYRIA

Nahariyya   1978

Haifa

ISRAEL
Boundaries per 1949
armistice with Arab
states

**GOLAN
HEIGHTS**
Isr. occ. 1967,
annexed 1981

L. Tiberias

Annexed by Jordan
1950; occ. by Israel
1967–2005; partial
withdrawal 1997;
Arafat dies 2004; Abbas
new president 2005

**Tel Aviv-
Yafo**

**WEST
BANK**

Amman

Jerusalem
Consolidated
by Israel 1967

GAZA STRIP
Occ. by Israel
1956–57; 1967–2005

JORDAN
Brief federation
with Iraq 1958; civil
war 1970–71

Gaza

Dead
Sea

Port Said
Anglo-French invasion
and withdrawal 1956

Beersheba

Ismailia

Suez Canal   Nationalized by Egypt 1956;
canal closed 1967–75

EGYPT
Cease-fire lines 1973

Gidi Pass

Mitla Pass

Suez

Būr Tawfīq

Bitter
Lakes

Negev

**U.N.
PARTITION
PLAN
1947**

U.N.
Admin.

**Arab
State**

**Jewish
State**

A.
J.

A.

Sinai

Occupied by Israel 1956–57,
1967–74; phased evacuation
completed by 1982

G. of Suez

Elat

**Al
'Aqabah**

Gulf of
Aqaba

**SAUDI
ARABIA**

MEDITERRANEAN SEA

© HAMMOND W.A.C.

Main map labels

KAZAKHSTAN
Bishkek
UZBEKISTAN   Shymkent   KYRGYZSTAN
TASHKENT   Namangan
Andijon
Kashi
Aydar Köli   CHINA
Samarqand   TAJIKISTAN
RKMENISTAN   Dushanbe
Ashgabat
Mashhad
Kabul   Peshāwar   Srinagar
Islāmābād   KASHMIR   KASHMIR
Capital 1967   Rāwalpindi

Soviets invade Afghanistan
following power struggles
among leftists 1979–80;
Soviet troops withdrawn 1989

Kashmir region in dispute between India
and Pakistan since 1947; cease-fire 1949;
intermittent conflict 1965

JAMMU

AZAD   AND

AFGHANISTAN
Monarchy overthrown 1973; leftist military coup 1978;
widespread Muslim guerilla resistance 1978–2001;
U.S. Military strike ousts Taliban, interim government
established 2001; New president elected 2004

Soviet troops withdrawn
ist coup 1953, rule of shah 1953–79;
demonstrations and rioting
eocratic state established 1979

LAHORE
Kandahār   Faisalābād   Ludhiāna
Islamic republic 1956; Civil War
with East Pakistan (Bangladesh) 1971;
War with India 1971–72
Multān

Kerman
Quetta

Subcontinent partitioned between Hindu India
and Muslim Pakistan 1947; over 1,000,000 killed
in rioting; millions of both communities forced
to flee in crisscross migration

Over 26,000 killed in
Bam earthquake 2003   Zāhedān
Bīkaner
Nuclear testing 1998, 2002

PAKISTAN
1947

INDIA
Jaipur

Bandar 'Abbās

Ra's al Khaymah
Joined U.A.E. 1972

Hyderābād
Udaipur

Str. of
Hormuz

bayy
Gwādar
Ceded to Pakistan
by Oman 1958
KARĀCHI
Former Capital
AHMADĀBĀD
Vadodara

Gulf of
Oman   Muscat

bal Jabal al Akhdar

OMAN
(formerly
at and Oman)

bal revolt
455–59   1953

1977

Jazirat
Maşirah
Emergency base
available to U.S.

Kuria Muria Is.
Ceded to Oman by
Britain 1967

ARABIAN

SEA

© HAMMOND WORLD ATLAS CORPORATION

1900-1919

1900 The Ottoman Empire stretches from what is now Libya to the Persian Gulf. It includes Egypt, parts of Arabia and the Balkans, Palestine, Syria and Iraq.
1901 Petroleum is discovered in Persia.
1902 Ibn Saud conquers Riyadh, beginning a lengthy campaign to unite central Arabia.
1906 JAN—Algeciras Conference establishes a French-Spanish police force to guard Moroccan ports.
1907 AUG 31—British-Russian agreement guarantees independent Afghanistani sphere of British influence.
1908 JUL 24—Young Turk revolution in Macedonia forces Turkish Sultan Abdul Hamid II to restore 1876 constitution.
1911 OCT 3—Italian troops capture Tripoli, beginning the seizure of Libya from the Turks.
1912 MAR 30—Treaty of Fez establishes French protectorate of Morocco.
OCT 19—Ottoman Empire cedes Libya to Italy.
OCT 19—Bulgaria, Greece, Serbia and Montenegro attack Turkish-held areas of eastern Europe.
NOV 27—Spanish protectorate is created in northern Morocco.
1913 MAY 30—Treaty of London ends Balkan-Turkish fighting, with loss of Turkish territory in Europe.
1914 AUG 2—Turks agree with Germany to enter World War I on the side of the Central Powers.
DEC 18—As war begins, British establish protectorates over Egypt and Kuwait, and annex Cyprus.
1915 APR 25—British troops establish beachheads on Gallipoli Peninsula in Turkey.
1916 JAN 9—British Gallipoli Campaign ends in failure.
JUN 5—Sharif Hussein ibn Ali leads revolt against Turks in Arabia, capturing Mecca in five days. Hussein proclaims himself King of Arab countries in October.
NOV 3—Qatar becomes a British protectorate.
1917 NOV 2—British Foreign Minister Arthur Balfour supports proposed Jewish homeland in Palestine.
NOV 7—Turks retreat in 3rd Battle of Giza against British.
DEC 9—British forces capture Jerusalem.
1918 OCT 1—British take Damascus.
OCT 5—French capture Beirut. Anticipating end of Ottoman rule, Emir Faisal proclaims a Syrian state.
OCT 31—Armistice ends Middle East fighting after Turkish forces are surrounded at Sharqat.
1919 MAY—Turkish War of Independence begins in Samsun under Mustafa Kemal.

1920-1939

1920 APR 20—Turkish nationalists set up a provisional government in Ankara.
APR 26—San Remo Conference approves mandates for former territories of the Ottoman Empire. Great Britain will administer Mesopotamia (Iraq) and Palestine, while France is given mandate over Syria, including Lebanon.
AUG 10—Sultan Mohammed VI accepts Treaty of Sèvres, which imposes harsh terms upon the defeated Ottoman Empire. Alternative Kemal government in Ankara refuses to sign the treaty.
1921 FEB 21—Reza Khan seizes Tehran and establishes a new government.
APR 1—Britain splits Palestine mandate, creating Transjordan, under rule of Abdullah of the Hashemites.
AUG 23—Faisal is proclaimed king of Iraq, two months after fleeing from the French in Syria.
1922 Southern border of Kuwait is established with the Kingdom of Najd (Saudi Arabia), including a Neutral Zone between the two countries.
FEB 28—Egypt becomes an independent monarchy.
1923 JUL 24—The Treaty of Lausanne is signed by Turkey. It nullifies claims to Egypt, Sudan and Cyprus, but is less harsh than Treaty of Sèvres, allowing Turkey to retain Thrace, Kurdistan and Armenia, in return for open passage through the Bosporus and Dardanelles.
OCT 23—Turkey is declared a republic by Kemal (later called Ataturk).
1924 King Ibn Saud of Najd ousts King Hussein from Mecca.
1925 MAY 1—Cyprus becomes a British Crown Colony.
DEC 12—The 131-year Kajar dynasty ends as Reza Shah Pahlavi (Khan) is proclaimed shah of Persia.
DEC 16—League of Nations awards Mosul area to Iraq.

1929 OCT 16—Amir Habibullah assumes throne in Afghanistan.
1932 SEP 23—The Kingdom of Saudi Arabia is decreed by Ibn Saud.
OCT 23—Iraq gains independence.
1934 In Tunisia, Habib Bourguiba founds New Constitution party, presses for independence.
1935 MAR 21—Shah Pahlavi changes the name of Persia to Iran.
1936 Commercial quantities of crude oil are discovered in Saudi Arabia.
SEP 9—Syrian-French treaty secures separate status for Lebanon.
1938 NOV 10—Ataturk dies. He is succeeded as president of Turkey by Ismet Inonu.
1939 DEC 27—Earthquakes and floods leave over 30,000 dead in the Anatolia region of Turkey.

1940-1959

1940 SEP 13—Italy invades Egypt from Libya.
1941 JAN 22—British forces rout Italian troops at Tobruk, Libya.
FEB 12—German Field Marshall Erwin Rommel arrives in Libya to begin the Axis offensive in north Africa.
MAY 31—British forces retake Baghdad, ousting a short-lived pro-German insurgent government.
SEP 16—Reza Shah abdicates the Iranian throne in favor of Mohammed Reza Pahlavi, his eldest son.
1942 JAN 29—Tripartite Treaty between U.S.S.R., Great Britain and Iran allows outside occupation of Iran for the duration of World War II.
JUN 21—Rommel's forces capture Tobruk.
NOV 5—British forces, under Gen. Bernard Montgomery, send German armor into retreat at El Alamein, Egypt.
NOV 8—British and American forces land in Morocco and Algeria.
1943 MAY 13—Axis forces in north Africa surrender in Tunis.
NOV 22—Lebanon attains independence from France.
1944 JAN 1—Syria achieves independence from France.
1945 MAR 22—Egypt, Iraq, Lebanon, Saudi Arabia, Syria, Yemen and Transjordan form the Arab League.
1946 MAY—Soviet troops withdraw from Iran, after Iran grants oil concessions to the U.S.S.R.
MAY 22—Britain relinquishes mandate of Transjordan. King Abdullah is first ruler.
DEC—Pro-Soviet separatist regimes collapse in Azerbaijani and Kurdistani regions of Iran.
1947 AUG 15—The state of Pakistan is created, ending nearly a century of British control.
NOV 29—United Nations partition plan, rejected by the Arab League, divides Palestine into a Jewish and an Arab state.
1948 MAY 14—Nation of Israel is proclaimed; David Ben-Gurion is prime minister. Armed forces from Egypt, Transjordan, Syria and Lebanon begin invasion.
1949 APR 3—Last Israeli-Arab armistice is signed with the newly-named Hashemite Kingdom of Jordan.
1950 APR 24—Jordan annexes 2,000 square miles of West Bank area it has controlled since the 1948-9 war.
1951 JUL 20—King Abdullah of Jordan is assassinated.
DEC 24—Libya gains independence as British and French areas are united. Muhammad Idris is proclaimed king.
1952 FEB 18—Turkey is admitted as a member of the North Atlantic Treaty Organization (NATO).
JUL 23—A military coup, led by Gamal Abdel Nasser, deposes Egyptian King Farouk.
1953 MAY 2—King Hussein becomes ruler of Jordan.
NOV 9—Ibn Saud dies and is succeeded as King of Saudi Arabia by his eldest son, Saud.
1954 NOV 1—Guerrilla attacks in the mountains of Algeria signal the start of armed rebellion against French control.
1956 JAN 1—Sudan is declared an independent republic, ending 57 years of joint British-Egyptian administration.
MAR 2-Morocco gains independence from France.
MAR 9-Archbishop Makarios is exiled from Cyprus for his demands for the unification of Cyprus with Greece.
MAR 20—Tunisia gains independence from France.
JUL 26—Egypt nationalizes the Suez Canal company to fund Aswan High Dam project after U.S. and U.K. funding is withdrawn.
OCT 29—Israel invades Egypt, reaching the Suez Canal.
NOV 6—A U.N. cease-fire is reached, but final evacuation of Suez Canal zone does not take place until December 22nd.
1957 JUL 25—Tunisian monarchy is abolished. Bourguiba is named president of the new republic.

1958 FEB 22—Syria and Egypt form the United Arab Republic.
JUL 14—Iraqi Army overthrows King Faisal II.
JUL 15—U.S. Marines land in Lebanon as a show of force to quiet Muslim-Christian civil strife.
NOV 17—Lt. Gen. Ibrahim Abboud overthrows the government of Sudan.

1960-1979

1960 MAY 27—Turkish Army overthrows the government.
AUG 16—Cyprus becomes an independent republic. Archbishop Makarios, who returned from exile in 1959, is elected president.
SEP—Organization of Petroleum Exporting Countries (OPEC) is formed by Iraq, Iran, Kuwait, Saudi Arabia and Venezuela.
1961 FEB 26—Moroccan King Mohammed V dies. His son, Hassan II, succeeds him, resulting in a parliamentary constitution the next year.
JUN 19—Kuwait gains independence. British troops thwart an Iraqi attempt to annex Kuwait.
SEP 28—Syria withdraws from the U.A.R.
1962 MAR 18—Cease-fire between France and National Liberation Front (F.L.N.) ends guerrilla war in Algeria.
APR 2—Monarchies form Federation of South Arabia.
JUL 3—France declares Algeria independent.
SEP 28—Establishment of the Yemen Arab Republic is aided by Egyptian military. Civil war begins versus royalists, aided by Saudi Arabia.
1963 JAN 18—Former British colony of Aden joins Federation of South Arabia.
FEB 9—A military junta takes control of Iraq.
SEP 8—Voters approve a constitution for Algeria. Ahmed Ben Bella is elected president later in the month.
1964 MAY—Palestine Liberation Organization (PLO) is established in Jerusalem.
AUG 9—A cease-fire ends eight months of warfare between Greek and Turkish factions on Cyprus.
NOV 2—King Saud is deposed and Faisal becomes King of Saudi Arabia.
1965 JUN 19—Revolutionary Council topples the Algerian government in bloodless coup. Ben Bella is confined for 15 years.
1967 MAY—U.N. forces withdraw from the Israeli border. Egypt closes the Gulf of Aqaba to Israeli shipping.
JUN 5—Israeli surprise attacks destroy surrounding Arab countries air forces. Six-Day War victory gains Israel control of the Gaza Strip, Sinai Peninsula, West Bank and Golan Heights. Egypt closes Suez Canal.
NOV 30—As British forces leave Aden, South Arabian government is overthrown by leftists. People's Republic of South Yemen is declared.
1968 JUL 17—Revolutionary Command Council takes control of Iraq under Ahmad Hasan al-Bakr.
NOV—Cypriot National Guard attacks Turkish enclaves, leading to the brink of war. Hostilities end when Greek troops leave the island.
1969 MAY 25—A military coup, under Col. Jaafar al-Nimeiri, takes control of Sudan.
SEP 1—Monarchy in Libya is overthrown. Military coup is led by Col. Muammar al-Qaddafi.
DEC 18—Kuwait and Saudi Arabia formally divide the Neutral Zone between their countries.
1970 JUL 23—Said Bin Taimur, Sultan of Muscat and Oman, is overthrown by his son, Qabus Ibn Saud.
AUG 9—Muscat and Oman is renamed the Sultinate of Oman.
SEP 6—Palestinian radicals begin hijacking of four airliners. Three are held in Jordan, then blown up.
SEP 16—Martial law declared in Jordan as civil strife breaks out. Syrian tanks intervene on behalf of Palestinians, but are ousted after ten days.
SEP 28—Egyptian Pres. Nasser dies of a heart attack; succeeded by Anwar Sadat.
NOV 13—Lt. Gen. Hafez al-Assad leads a bloodless takeover of the Syrian government.
DEC 1—Radical forces take over South Yemen, renaming the country the People's Democratic Republic of Yemen.
1971 JUL—In northern Jordan, King Hussein's army destroys last remaining Palestinian guerrilla strongholds.
AUG 14—Bahrain gains independence.
SEP 1—Qatar becomes an independent state.
DEC 2—Six of the Trucial States form the United Arab Emirates. Ras al Khaimah joins in 1972.
1972 NOV 21—Israel and Syria clash in heaviest fighting since 1967 War.
1973 JUL 17—In Afghanistan, a military coup ousts King Zahir Shah. Sardar Mohammad Daoud declares himself president of a new republic.
OCT 6—Egypt and Syria attack Israel on Yom Kippur. Israeli forces counterattack, cross the Suez Canal, and recapture the Golan Heights.

OCT 17—Arab states embargo oil shipments to the U.S.
OCT 27—U.N. peacekeeping forces arrive in Cairo.
NOV 11—Egypt and Israel sign a cease-fire agreement.
1974 MAR 4—Israel returns control of the Suez Canal to Egypt.
MAR 18—Arab nations end U.S. oil embargo.
APR 11—Israeli Premier Golda Meir resigns as fighting rages with Syria in the Golan Heights.
MAY 31—Syria and Israel sign an accord, ending hostilities.
JUL 15—Cypriot Pres. Makarios ousted at the instigation of Greece. Five days later, Turkish forces land on Cyprus.
AUG 16—Turkey declares cease-fire after gaining over a third of Cyprus.
NOV 13—U.N. affirms Palestinian sovereignty and right of self-determination within Palestine.
1975 MAR 25—Saudi King Faisal is assassinated, and succeeded by his half-brother, Crown Prince Khalid.
APR—Political and religious conflict in Lebanon escalates into civil war.
JUN 5—Suez Canal reopens after eight year closure.
NOV 6—Morocco's King Hassan II claims Spanish-held Western Sahara, as 40,000 unarmed civilians cross the border in the "Green March".
NOV 21—Spanish leave Western Sahara. Morocco and Mauritania administer the territory until 1979, when Mauritania abandons its claim.
1976 MAY—Syrian troops intervene in Lebanon.
1977 JUL 21—Border clashes between Libya and Egypt escalate. Egypt accepts a truce four days later.
NOV 20—Egyptian Pres. Sadat becomes first Arab leader to visit Israel.
1978 MAR—Israel attacks PLO camps in southern Lebanon.
APR 27—Pres. Daoud is killed as Marxists seize the Afghanistan government. Conservatives begin nationwide guerrilla warfare.
1979 JAN 16—Mounting protests force Iran's Shah Mohammed Reza Pahlavi to flee his country.
FEB 1—Exiled religious leader Ayatollah Khomeini returns from France to Iran to establish the Islamic Republic.
MAR 26—Egypt and Israel sign peace accords. Egypt is suspended from Arab League membership.
JUL 16—Saddam Hussein assumes Iraqi presidency.
NOV 4—Militants take 52 hostages at U.S. Embassy in Tehran.
DEC 27—Soviet troops invade Afghanistan.

1980-1999

1980 APR 24—U.S. hostage rescue attempt in Iran ends in failure.
SEP 12—Military coup ousts the Turkish government.
SEP 17—Iraq claims the Shatt-al-Arab waterway.
SEP 22—Iraq invades Iran, beginning Eight Year War.
1981 JAN 20—Iran releases all American hostages.
JUN 7—Israeli planes destroy a partially-built nuclear reactor on the outskirts of Baghdad.
OCT 6—Sadat is assassinated in Egypt. Hosni Mubarak is his successor.
DEC 14—Israel annexes the Golan Heights. U.N. voids the annexation.
1982 APR 25—Israel completes Sinai withdrawal.
MAY 24—Iran recaptures its port city of Khorramshahr, taking 30,000 Iraqi prisoners.
JUN 6—Israel invades Lebanon to destroy PLO bases, advancing in four days to the outskirts of Beirut.
JUN 14—Saudi Arabia's King Khalid dies and is succeeded by his brother Crown Prince Fahd.
AUG 19—Ten-week siege of Beirut ends.
AUG 25—U.S. Marines enter Lebanon, then withdraw after PLO leaves Beirut.
SEP 14—Pres. Bashir Gemayel is assassinated in Lebanon. He is succeeded by his brother Amin.
SEP 15—Israel's Menachem Begin resigns due to poor health. Yitzhak Shamir succeeds him as prime minister.
SEP 18—Lebanese Christians massacre 300 Palestinian refugees.
SEP 29—U.S., French and Italian troops arrive in Beirut as Israel withdraws from the city.
NOV 7—A new constitution restores civilian rule in Turkey.
1983 APR 6—Sudanese military topples government of Pres. Nimeiri.
APR 18—Bomb blast destroys U.S. Embassy in Beirut. Radical Iranians claim responsibility.
SEP 26—Syria and Lebanon agree to a cease-fire in Beirut.
OCT 23—Terrorist attack on U.S. Marine barracks at Beirut Airport kills 241. Another 58 die in blast at French barracks.
NOV 15—Turkish Republic of Northern Cyprus is declared, dividing North and South. U.N. Security Council condemns the move.
DEC 20—Six-week Syrian siege of PLO ends as Yasir Arafat and 4,000 troops evacuate by sea.

1984 FEB 26—U.S. Marines withdraw from Lebanon.
MAY 20—Arab League condemns Iran's attack on Persian Gulf shipping.
JUN 5—Saudi jets down two Iranian planes over the Persian Gulf.
AUG 6—U.S. and British ships are sent to the Persian Gulf to clear mines. Russian, French and Italian ships arrive within weeks to help keep shipping lanes open.
1985 FEB 16—Israeli troops leave Sidon in withdrawal from Lebanon.
JUN 14—TWA airliner is seized in Beirut. Hostage ordeal ends 17 days later when Israel releases Shiite prisoners.
OCT 1—Israeli jets attack PLO headquarters in Tunisia.
OCT 7—Armed terrorists take over Italian cruise ship *Achille Lauro*. Hijackers are captured three days later on airline flight from Egypt.
1986 MAR 24—U.S. Navy exercises in the Gulf of Sidra draw attacks from Libyan jets and patrol boats.
APR 14—U.S. bombers attack military installations near Tripoli, Libya. Qaddafi's adopted daughter is killed.
1987 JAN 5—Afghanistan announces cease-fire agreement with rebels.
MAY 17—Iraqi missile hits *USS Stark* in Persian Gulf, killing 37. Iraq apologizes for the unintentional incident.
JUL 31—Rioting by pilgrims kills over 400 in Mecca.
SEP 15—U.S. attacks Iranian minelayer in the Gulf.
1st INTEFADA
OCT 16—Iranian missile strikes U.S.-flagged Kuwaiti tanker in Persian Gulf. U.S. shells offshore Iranian oil rig, used as gunboat base, three days later.
NOV 11—Arab leaders support Iraq in war with Iran.
1988 MAR 11—Iraqis repel Iranian attack on the town of Halabja with mustard and cyanide gasses.
JUN 7—PLO agrees to recognize Israel, in return for a Palestinian referendum.
JUN 13—Iran attacks oil fields near Basra, triggering one of the bloodiest battles in the war with Iraq.
JUL 3—*USS Vincennes* missile destroys an Iranian airliner over the Persian Gulf, killing 290. U.S. expresses regret and pays reparations to the victims' families.
JUL 31—Jordan relinquishes claim to the West Bank.
AUG 20—Eight-Year War between Iran and Iraq ends.
SEP 3—Kurds flee to Turkey as rebellion is crushed in northern Iraq.
SEP 22—Outgoing Lebanese President Gemayel appoints three Christians and three Muslims to interim military government.
NOV 15—Palestinian National Council (P.N.C.) proclaims an independent Palestinian state.
DEC 21—Pan Am Flight 103 explodes over Lockerbie, Scotland killing 270. Libyan officers are suspected of the bombing.
1989 JAN 30—Syria and Iran end dispute between rival Shiite factions in Lebanon, granting control of southern Lebanon to Syrian-backed Amal.
FEB 9—U.S.S.R. withdraws from Afghanistan.
MAY 21—Egypt rejoins the Arab League.
JUL 3—Iran's Ayatollah Khomeini dies.
JUL 29—Rafsanjani elected executive president of Iran.
AUG 13—Syrian tanks attack Christians in east Beirut.
SEP 19—UTA Airline flight 772 explodes over the Niger desert killing 170. Libyan officers are suspected of the bombing.
SEP 23—Cease-fire begins in Lebanon after Arab League plan is accepted by militant Christian Gen. Michel Aoun.
NOV 22—Lebanese Pres. Rene Moawad is assassinated 15 days after his election. Elias Hrawi succeeds him.
1990 MAR 14—Libyan factory is heavily damaged by fire a week after U.S. says it is used to make chemical weapons.
MAY 22—Republic of Yemen is created by merger of Yemen Arab Republic and People's Democratic Republic of Yemen.
JUL 2—1,400 pilgrims die in crowd stampede in Mecca.
AUG 2—Iraq invades Kuwait. Kuwaiti emir flees to Saudi Arabia. Iraqi forces mass along Saudi border.
AUG 6—U.N. condemns invasion of Kuwait and orders boycott of Iraq.
AUG 7—Multinational forces, led by U.S., begin buildup in Saudi Arabia.
AUG 8—Iraq claims initial annexation of Kuwait.
AUG 9—First U.S. forces arrive in Saudi Arabia. U.N. declares Iraqi annexation of Kuwait invalid.
AUG 12—U.S. begins naval blockade halting oil shipments from Iraq.
AUG 28—Iraq declares Kuwait its 19th province.
NOV 29—U.N. Security Council authorizes use of force against Iraq unless it withdraws from Kuwait by Jan. 1991.
DEC 6—Iraq frees foreign nationals held hostage.
1991 JAN 12—Congress grants Pres. George Bush authority to wage war against Iraq.
JAN 16—Massive air attack is launched against Iraq as multinational forces begin Operation Desert Storm.

JAN 17—Iraq begins missile attacks against Israel.
JAN 22—Iraq blows up Kuwaiti oil wells.
JAN 25—Iraq pumps over a million gallons of crude oil into Persian Gulf.
FEB 23—Allied forces begin ground assault on Iraq and occupied Kuwait.
FEB 27—Liberation of Kuwait is complete. Crushed Iraqi troops agree to allied terms ending Persian Gulf War.
MAR 3—Cease-fire agreed to by Allied and Iraqi leaders.
APR—Kurdish rebellion in northern Iraq is crushed as a million flee to Turkey. Many return after creation of a safe zone for refugees.
SEP 13—U.S. and former Soviet Union end military aid to rival factions in Afghanistan civil strife.
OCT 30—Arab-Israeli peace conference begins in Madrid with all parties in attendance for the first time since the establishment of Israel.
NOV 14—Allied investigators charge Libyan officers with engineering the Lockerbie bombing in 1988.
DEC 4—American journalist Terry Anderson is released by Islamic extremists. He's the last of nine hostages freed in Lebanon since August.
1992 FEB—Algerian military cancels elections, fearing a win by the fundamentalist Islamic Salvation Front.
APR 28—A coalition of Islamic rebels takes power from the communists in Afghanistan as civil war continues.
JUN 23—Labor party wins national elections in Israel.
JUN 29—Algerian President Boudiaf is assassinated.
AUG 27—U.S., British and French begin enforcing a "no-fly" zone in southern Iraq, preventing Iraqi air attacks against the Shiite population.
1993 MAR 7—Peace plan ending civil war in Afghanistan is signed in Islāmābād, Pakistan by eight factions.
MAR 27—Algeria ends ties with Iran, charging Iranian involvement in political assassinations in Algeria.
JUN 14—Tansu Ciller is named the first woman Prime Minister of Turkey.
AUG 18—U.S. accuses Sudan of terrorism and cancels aid.
AUG 25—U.S. trade sanctions are imposed on Pakistan because of their missile technology deals with China.
SEP 13—The PLO and Israel sign a peace accord in Washington, D.C. granting Palestinian autonomy in Gaza Strip, West Bank and East Jerusalem.
DEC 30—Israel begins diplomatic ties with The Vatican.
1994 JAN 30—High Security Council of Algeria appoints Defense Minister Lamine Zeroual interim President.
MAY 4—PLO assumes authority in Gaza Strip and town of Jericho, followed by Israeli withdrawal two weeks later.
JUL 7—Yemeni forces loyal to President Ali Abdullah Saleh capture Aden, ending nine weeks of civil strife.
OCT 7—Iraq deploys 20,000 troops to Kuwait border; U.S. troop response prompts Baghdad to withdraw.
OCT 26—Israel and Jordan formally end 46-year state-of-war.
NOV 10—Iraq recognizes sovereignty of Kuwait.
1995 MAY 8—U.S. suspends trade with Iran, citing support of terrorism and attempts to acquire nuclear weapons.
JUN 27—Shaikh Hamad Bin Khalifa al-Thani ousts his father as Amir of Qatar in a bloodless coup.
NOV 4—Israeli Prime Minister Yitzhak Rabin is assassinated by Yigal Amir, a Jewish religious extremist. Shimon Peres succeeds Rabin, vowing continued peace efforts.
NOV 16—Lamine Zeroual is elected Algerian president.
1996 JAN 20—Yasir Arafat is elected president of the Palestine National Authority (P.N.A.).
APR 26—Cease-fire ends eighteen days of fighting along the Lebanon-Israel border after over 150 are killed.
MAY 20—U.N. and Iraq sign an oil export agreement, voided Sept. 1 when Iraq seizes Kurdish town under U.N. protection.
MAY 29—Netanyahu elected prime minister of Israel.
1997 JAN 17—Israel withdraws from Hebron West Bank.
MAR 7—Israel gives partial control of West Bank to P.N.A.
1998 JAN 20—meetings are held in Washington D.C. to attempt to restart stalled peace process.
AUG 24—Netanyahu accepts U.S. proposal that Israel withdraw from portions of West Bank.
OCT 23—Wye River Memorandum (Wye Accord) reached regarding Israeli withdrawal from part of West Bank.
NOV 24—Gaza Int'l Airport opens in Gaza Strip.
DEC 21—Palestinians withhold support for Netanyahu's peacemaking policy. Israeli Knesset votes to dissolve and to hold early elections.
1999 JUL 6—Labor party's Ehud Barak replaces Netanyahu as Israeli Prime Minister.
OCT 12—General Pervez Musharraf seizes power in Pakistan.

2000-2006

2000   JAN 3—Israel and Syria resume peace talks in United States.

FEB 3—Peace summit breaks up over proposed Israeli withdrawal from West Bank under revised Wye Accord.

MAR 21—Israel surrenders West Bank territory to Palestinians as originally agreed in Wye Accord.

JUL 25—Camp David summit ends without peace agreement after two weeks of negotiations.

OCT 12—Islamic militant suicide bombing of destroyer *USS Cole* in Yemen kills 17 sailors. Osama bin Laden believed responsible.

OCT 17—Pres. Clinton heads summit in Egypt announcing plans to end Palestinian-Israeli violence. The plan fails soon after it is accepted.

DEC 10—Israeli Prime Minister Barak resigns.

2001   FEB 6—Ariel Sharon becomes Israel's prime minister.

MAR 12—World expresses outrage as Taliban in Afghanistan destroy ancient historical statues in Kabul Museum, historical sites in Ghazni and 2300-year-old Buddha statues in Bamiyan.

JUN 14—Israeli and Palestinian leaders agree to U.S. cease-fire plan.

JUL 31—Eight killed when Israeli missiles bomb offices of militant Islamic group Hamas.

AUG 9—Palestinian suicide bomber kills and wounds hundreds in Israeli restaurant.

AUG 13—Suspected Palestinian suicide bomber base is attacked by Israeli tanks.

SEP 11—Terrorists hijack four U.S. commercial jets and, using them as missiles, crash them into New York's World Trade Center and Washington D.C.'s Pentagon. Thousands die in Twin Towers' collapse and Pentagon's damage. Passengers storm cockpit of fourth plane, which crashes killing all aboard. Osama bin Laden held directly responsible for attacks.

OCT 7—After Taliban refuse to surrender Bin Laden, U.S. and U.K. launch air attack on Afghanistan.

NOV—Turkey threatens to annex north Cyprus if the south joins the European Union before a settlement between the two is reached.

DEC 5—Afghan political groups meet in Bonn, Germany and select Hamid Karzai chairman of interim government.

DEC 7—Taliban loses last major stronghold as opposition forces enter Kandahār.

2002   JAN 29—U.S. Pres. George W. Bush declares Iran, Iraq and North Korea an "Axis of Evil."

MAY—Political tensions increase between India and Pakistan over disputed Kashmir region.

MAY 25-28—Pakistan test fires three medium-range missiles capable of carrying nuclear warheads expanding political unrest in the Middle East.

JUN—Afghani Grand Council elects Karzai President of transitional government until elections are held in 2004.

JUL 6—Vice-President Haji Abdul Qadir killed by gunmen in Kabul.

SEP 5—Karzai narrowly escapes assassination in home town of Kandahār.

OCT 16—Bush signs U.S. Joint Resolution 114 authorizing use of military force against Iraq.

NOV—U.N. inspectors resume search for hidden Weapons of Mass Destruction in Iraq.

DEC—U.S. rejects declaration that Iraq has no current WMD programs.

2003   JAN—U.N. inspector Blix reports finding no evidence of Iraq reviving its nuclear weapons program.

MAR 1—U.N. supervised disposal of Iraq's Al-Samoud II missiles begins.

MAR 17—Bush demands Hussein and his sons leave Iraq within 48 hours or face military action.

MAR 19—Military action (Operation Iraqi Freedom) to disarm Iraq begins.

MAR 20—Turkey refuses use of air bases for U.S. military action, but allows use of airspace, and authorizes dispatch of troops into Kurdish Iraq.

APR 9—Coalition forces enter Baghdad and topple statue of Hussein in central square.

APR 21—Coalition Provisional Authority established as temporary government of Iraq.

MAY 1—Bush declares end to major combat operations in Iraq.

JUN 15—U.S. launches Operation Desert Scorpion to defeat Iraqi resistance against coalition troops.

JUL 13—Interim Iraqi Governing Council formed to draft new constitution.

JUL 22—Hussain's sons Uday and Qusay killed by U.S. forces in Mosul.

AUG—Libya accepts responsibility for the Lockerbie bombing and agrees to compensate families of the victims.

SEP 12—The International Atomic Energy Agency insists Iran prove it is not pursuing an atomic weapons program.

SEP 12—U.N. Security Council votes to lift sanctions against Libya imposed since Lockerbie bombing.

OCT 2—Iraq Survey Group head David Kay tells U.S. congressional committee no WMD's have been found.

OCT 21—Iran claims it is suspending uranium enrichment program and will allow U.N. to inspect nuclear facilities.

NOV—IAEA inspectors determine Iran has no nuclear weapons program.

NOV 25—Cease-fire instituted between Pakistan and India.

DEC—Pakistani President Musharraf survives two assassination attempts by Islamic extremists.

DEC 13—U.S. forces capture Saddam Hussein near his hometown of Tikrit.

DEC 19—Libya agrees to abandon its WMD development programs.

DEC 26—Earthquake strikes Bam in southeast Iran leaving thousands dead and injured. International rescue teams from at least 21 countries, including U.S., respond to disaster relief.

2004   JAN 1—Relationship between India and Pakistan improves as air and surface transportation are reestablished between the two countries.

JAN 9—Libya accepts responsibility for the UTA Airline bombing and agrees to compensate families of the victims.

JAN 16—Afghani Grand Council adopts constitution creating a republic.

MAR 8—Interim constitution signed by Iraqi Governing Council.

APR 23—U.S. lifts most economic sanctions against Libya imposed since Lockerbie bombing.

APR 24—Referendums on whether to accept a U.N. plan for reunification pass in southern part of Cyprus but fail in north.

MAY 1—Southern Cyprus joins EU as a divided state despite failed reunification with the north.

MAY 5—Accusations of abuse by U.S. military of Iraqi detainees held at Abu Graib prison is confirmed.

MAY 28—Former Baath party member Iyad Allawi named Prime Minister of Iraqi interim government.

JUN 28—U.N Security Council transfers full sovereignty to interim Iraqi government.

JUN 28—U.S. resumes direct diplomatic ties with Libya.

JUN 30—U.S. transfers legal custody of Hussein to Iraqi government.

AUG 10—Libya agrees to compensate families and victims of Berlin nightclub bombing in 1986.

OCT 9—Landmark presidential elections held in Afghanistan.

OCT 24—Interim leader Karzai wins Afghan presidential election with 55.4% of the vote.

NOV 11—Arafat dies in French hospital.

DEC 7—Karzai sworn in as Afghan president.

DEC 17—EU leaders begin official membership negotiations with Turkey.

2005   JAN 9—Mahmoud Abbas wins a majority in the Palestinian presidential election.

JAN 30—Despite election day attacks, 58% of Iraqi citizens participate in the first multiparty elections in over 50 years. Iraqis vote for provincial parliament members and a National Assembly to write Iraq's constitution.

JAN 30—U.S. oil companies return to Libya after 20 year absence.

FEB 8—At an Egyptian summit, Sharon and Abbas agree to a truce ending over four years of incessant fighting between Israel and Palestine.

FEB 20—Israeli cabinet approves plan for removal of Jewish settlements from Gaza Strip and part of West Bank.

APR 5—Transitional assembly selects Jalal Talabani as Iraqi president.

APR 7—Talabani chooses Ibrahim al-Jaafari prime minister of Iraq.

APR 28—National Assembly approves cabinet, creating first freely elected government in Iraqi history.

APR 30—After more than twenty years, Syria restores diplomatic relations with Iraq.

MAY 26—Abbas gets U.S. support for settlement plan. Israel releases 400 prisoners and promises to withdraw from Palestinian cities in West Bank.

AUG 1—Saudi Arabia's King Fahd dies and is succeeded by Crown Prince Abdullah.

AUG 24—Israeli evacuation of Gaza and West Bank completed.

OCT 4—EU leaders begin official membership negotiations with Turkey.

OCT 9—First parliamentary and provincial elections in more than 30 years held in Afghanistan.

NOV 10—Explosions kill more than 50 and injure 300 at hotels in Amman, Jordan. Al-Qaeda based suicide bombers are suspected.

NOV 28—Hussein trial for crimes against humanity begins in Iraq.

2006   JAN 4—Despite serious illness of Sharon, plans for March elections in Israel remain unchanged.

JAN 25—Islamic militant group Hamas wins surprise victory in Palestinian parliamentary elections.

Index to the Middle East and Northern Africa